contents

Out of the night that covers me,
  Black as the Pit from pole to pole,
I thank whatever gods may be
  For my unconquerable soul.

In the fell clutch of circumstance
  I have not winced nor cried aloud.
Under the bludgeonings of chance
  My head is bloody, but unbowed.

Beyond this place of wrath and tears
  Looms but the Horror of the shade,
And yet the menace of the years
  Finds, and shall find, me unafraid.

It matters not how strait the gate,
  How charged with punishments the scroll,
I am the master of my fate:
  I am the captain of my soul.

— "Invictus," William Ernest Henley
(1849–1903)

a WORD FROM
Kim Myles

When I was a teenager, I had one dream — to make it big in business by using my creativity and talent. I didn't know exactly *how* I could make this happen, but I was certain that I would need to work hard to make my dream come true.

I asked those people I admired most — people who'd achieved the success I was seeking — what it takes to make it, and they gave me some excellent advice and direction. Here's what I learned: To become highly successful in business, you need five main things: 1) creativity; 2) intelligence; 3) the ability to articulate clearly; 4) people who are in your corner and looking out for your best interests; and, perhaps most important, 5) a solid business plan.

I knew I already had four out of five in the bag: I'm good at coming up with fresh ideas. I'm a fairly smart person. I'm lucky enough to have been blessed with the ability to express myself, and, people, I *know* I've got style — "Myles" of it! I present myself well. Plus, I have a family who loves me, so I'm supported in many ways.

The one thing missing was a plan. What I lacked were the nuts-and-bolts details for beginning and then building a company. I needed a blueprint for success as a business owner.

I'd heard the term *entrepreneur*, but I didn't really know what it meant. Some of you might recognize it from your language classes: Entrepreneur is a French word that, roughly translated, refers to someone who takes on an enterprise.

I love this definition because it reminds me of moving ahead on a big journey, where I'm at the wheel — or captain of the starship!

I grew up in Bakersfield, California, a place just like most small towns in America. When I was 13 years old, I took my first step toward entrepreneurship. Once I'd done my research, my first attempt at business involved crafting and selling miniature decorative furniture to posh interior design boutiques.

The dollhouse-scale furniture was inspired by the fairy in the book *The Velveteen Rabbit*. The line included tiny thrones, canopy beds, and bassinets made of twigs and adorned with dried flower petals. The items were purely decorative and whimsical, meant to be tucked on a bookshelf or on top of a dresser. Buyers felt the pieces made unique display items and conversation pieces.

Then, throughout high school, I made and sold all kinds of items to local businesses. I created hand-painted flowerpots, funky hats, and chewy chocolate brownies, just to name a few. Basically, if I thought it was cool, I took the initiative to make

it and sell it. Juggling homework and a part-time job could sometimes be hard, but I learned that a true entrepreneur is someone who believes strongly in herself and doesn't give up when the going gets tough.

Now that I'm grown-up — and thanks to winning HGTV's *Design Star*, an interior design competition in which the victor gets her own TV show on the network (perhaps you've seen me on the small screen, fabricating *fabulous* rooms?) — I have the privilege of working as a professional interior designer, and hosting my own national television show. This forum allows me to continue to develop my ideas about design and my belief in my own style. In a nutshell, I strive to mix all kinds of cultural influences from all over the planet with the chicness of modern city living: a trend I call Global Urban Elegance.

Funny thing is, my own map to success has never followed a straight line. I've explored many options along the way, like acting, hairdressing, and set design. Though, on the surface, all of these things might seem to differ widely from one another, they have each played a major role in my current success on television. And, when you think about it, there is a common thread running through my many career paths: a love of beautiful things, presented dramatically, whether as a breathtaking stage scenario or stunning highlights!

Back when I was 13, crafting those crazy-cute pieces of minifurniture, who would have guessed I'd end up hosting my own interior design show? So take it from me: Don't be discouraged if your own journey leads you to unexplored

and unexpected places! Use each new experience (even the difficult ones) to learn and grow. As long as you stay both focused and open, you'll be more than fine.

One of the great gifts of my job is getting to meet a lot of young people who have goals similar to my own. I always tell them about NFTE. The Network for Teaching Entrepreneurship provides teens with that essential point number 5 I was missing: the proper blueprint for launching and running a successful company, even if you're still in school. What's really awesome is that many of the young people I meet in my professional travels are natural-born entrepreneurs to begin with, who have the added benefit of an organization such as NFTE right in their own classrooms. As you read this book, you'll learn more about NFTE and how to take advantage of what this important organization has to offer. And you'll also read the incredible, inspiring stories of teens just like you who had a business plan, put it into action, and ended up finalists for a $10,000 prize.

To those of you who, like me when I was a teen, want to make it big in business, my advice is a wholehearted "Go for it!" Building a dynamic future for yourself can be one of the best adventures of your life. But like anyone embarking on a voyage, don't hit the road without the right map to guide you — without your own personal GPS system. After all, you can't drive off into the sunset without a learner's permit! And make sure you strap on your seat belt for when you veer off the road or even run into the small-business version of a fender bender (which has happened to me plenty of times,

and happens to everyone who's brave enough to pursue their dreams). You can survive many minor crashes with the right support system.

The strongest net to catch you, hold you, and keep you safe is woven from the fabric of those things you probably already possess; those same five things that my mentors always listed, and which have been essential to my own success. Believe in your own power — your creativity and intelligence. Speak truth to this power — spread your message. Surround yourself with people who love, support, and can guide you. Then take the time to develop a plan of action.

The rest will follow. . . .

TO STUDENTS

from

Steve Mariotti

FOUNDER OF THE NETWORK FOR TEACHING ENTREPRENEURSHIP

This book has been designed to introduce you to the exciting world of being an entrepreneur. I hope that what you learn here will help you achieve financial independence and personal satisfaction. Knowing how business works will be of great value in any future career path you may take.

Learning the principles of entrepreneurship will teach you about more than just business and money, however. In this book, you will learn, among other things, how to negotiate, calculate return on investment, perform cost/benefit analysis, and keep track of your income and expenses. These skills apply to your personal as well as your business life. Even if you don't become a lifelong entrepreneur, learning how to start and operate a small business will give you an understanding of the business world that will make it much easier for you to get jobs and create a fulfilling career for yourself, and thus own your future.

The characteristics of the successful entrepreneur — a positive mental attitude, the ability to recognize opportunities

where others only see problems, and openness to creative solutions — are qualities worth developing. They will help you perform better in any situation life throws at you.

Owning your future will be the key to happiness. You can do so much good for your family, friends, and community by being aware of the opportunities and resources around you. Entrepreneurship is a way to do that — to make your dreams come true and help support the goals of those you care about. What you can learn from this book can help you make good personal decisions for the future. NFTE is here to support you. I hope you will visit our website at www.nfte.com. Good luck!

Sincerely yours,

Steve Mariotti
Founder, NFTE

TEN9EIGHT—
Game On!

On a day in late October 2008, a select group of teens gathered in New York City for one of the fiercest contests ever.

They were about to face a panel of the most distinguished and tough-minded judges. These kids were not there to see who would be the best singer — though many in the audience sang their praises. This was not a contest to find America's next top chef, model, or fashion designer — though lots of the contestants were model students who used their charm and ingenuity to win over the judges; and some of them did whip up their entries in the kitchen!

This was the final championship round of the Oppenheimer Funds/NFTE National Youth Entrepreneurship Challenge.

Through local, regional, and state NFTE competitions, these contestants had risen to the top of 24,000 competitors, and were now competing among 35 finalists.

At the national competition, there were 50 judges through several elimination rounds. The judges were among the most highly respected and successful business owners in the country. During the final rounds of competition, there were seven judges.

Their mission was to help find the nation's next great entrepreneur. Someone who, like themselves, had created a winning business and had successfully developed the key elements to make their ventures take off.

For one full day — fourteen long hours — these young women and men presented their most polished plans for everything from who would actually buy what they had to offer to how much money their companies would earn over a period of years. Each one of them was dressed to impress. Each had about eight minutes for their presentations. Then they were to face the judges for three solid minutes, while the judges hammered away at them with questions about their profits, strategic plans, return on investment, and customer base — terms the teen entrepreneurs had become very familiar with over the many months each spent building his or her business.

The stakes were some of the highest they'd ever known: a cash prize of $10,000 to start a company, and national media exposure that would put their products and services in front of millions.

In the next few pages, you'll come face-to-face with some incredible individuals — kids just like you — who wowed the judges with their brainpower, perseverance, and passion. And who showed them their business smarts by presenting their plans for launching and building their own companies.

Just as exciting, through the individual stories of these exceptional young people, you'll learn the important aspects of entrepreneurship and discover what it really takes to launch and run a business. Some of these teens had already beat incredible personal odds, and now they were about to use their fortitude to accomplish even greater feats.

Through these teens, you'll discover what makes a good

idea. You'll find out if you need to be rich to start a business, and what skills it takes to succeed.

A word of warning: This is not a competition for weaklings. Even to read about it, you'll want every ounce of strength you can summon. Like the contestants and judges themselves, you'll need focus and a solid backbone to determine who is most fit to win in business. If you haven't started biting your nails yet, get ready.

To figure out the winner, and to find out if you, too, have what it takes to be a champion in business, there are some thought-provoking questions to ask yourself.

Most definitely, you'll want to know who will walk away with bags of cash and a dream come true. But more than the big money is the big chance to offer people a quality product or service. And the opportunity to learn how to best meet a market need. The kids in this book will show you all of this and more as they share their experience, strength, and hope — as well as their insider tips and top secrets.

Featured in guest appearances throughout each teen's story are their parents, teachers, relatives, and friends, who all offer insights on what makes the students tick and why they have what it takes to be business owners.

The panel of judges will give you their behind-the-scenes views, revealing why one student's business might be special while another might be destined to flop. Budding "teenpreneurs," take note! This info is like gold: Not even the finalists themselves got to hear the judges' opinions during the contest. All they knew was that they were standing under

the hot lights and cameras of competition.

Once all the contestants had presented their individual business plans, the judges narrowed the pool to the three finalists, and ultimately chose the grand-prize winner.

As you read through the finalists' stories, you can judge, too, based on your own assessment of them and how much their business ideas appeal to you.

Over the course of the competition, the contestants were followed by a documentary film crew, their stories and that of this unforgettable contest to be showcased in a movie called *TEN9EIGHT: Shoot For the Moon*. (The judges' comments on each contestant are a composite drawn from their collective opinions as expressed in this film.) Lights, camera, action, the pressure was on, big-time! Like the countdown to the launch of a rocket ship — *10, 9, 8 . . .* — these contestants were ready to blast off into a galaxy of accomplishment. All of them were winners, but only one of them claimed the cash! Only one walked away with a grand prize that would finance their business endeavor.

Get ready to meet some of the brightest teens on this planet or any other! Kids with determination and desire. Kids who are a lot like you.

WHO WAS THE BIG WINNER?
THE CLOCK IS TICKING; THE COUNTDOWN IS ON.
TO FIND OUT, READ ON.

meet the JUDGes

Ken Banks
President and CEO
Banks Contracting Company

David P. Fialkow
Co-Founder and Managing Director
General Catalyst Partners

Wycliffe "Wyc" Grousbeck
Managing Partner, Governor, and CEO
Boston Celtics

Kay Koplovitz
Founder of USA Network
Chairman and CEO of Koplovitz & Co. LLC

David Pfeffer
Senior Vice President and CFO
OppenheimerFunds, Inc.

Ralph L. Schlosstein
Co-Founder and Former President, BlackRock
CEO, HighView Investment Group

Tom Scott
Co-Founder
Nantucket Nectars and Plum Television

meet the contestants

Tatyana Blackwell, 17

Just Cheer Uniforms
Capitol Heights, Maryland

Jessica Cervantes, 18

Popsy Cakes
Miami, Florida

Gabriel Echoles, 18, and Rodney Walker, 18

Forever Life Music & Video
Productions
Chicago, Illinois

Macalee Harlis, Jr., 19

MAC Shields
Fort Lauderdale, Florida

Shan Shan Huang, 19

Charger Station
Boston, Massachusetts

Amanda Loyola, 15

EcoDog Treats LLC
New York, New York

William Mack, 16, and Ja'Mal Wills, 17

J&W Sensations
Baltimore, Maryland

Robbie Martin, 17

The Deaf Academy
New Bedford, Massachusetts

Alexander Niles, 16

Niles Custom Guitars
Miami, Florida

"TO BE A GOOD ENTREPRENEUR, IT TAKES YOU BELIEVING IN YOURSELF, EVEN IF NOBODY ELSE DOES."

CHAPTER 1

CHEER CHAMP

Tatyana Blackwell

17

JUST CHEER UNIFORMS

Capitol Heights, Maryland

Tatyana's passion for cheerleading started when she was in the first grade. As a kid, she loved to watch the older girls who were on her school's cheerleading squad. Even though she was too young to be an official cheerleader, Tatyana sat down front to get a good look as the cheerleaders came out onto the basketball court or football field, where they would get the teams' players and their fans psyched for a big game. Tatyana learned quickly that to be a good cheerleader you need to be able to yell loudly, smile big, jump high, and spell the words that shout your team to success — V-I-C-T-O-R-Y! G-O! F-I-G-H-T!

Ever since Tatyana was old enough to yell — and spell — she was letting her school spirit show by cheering alongside the big kids who were making it happen. By the time Tatyana got to Suitland High School, she was R-E-A-D-Y to give the shout-out for her school's teams, which she did, with the pride and style of a cheerleading pro.

But there was one thing that stopped Tatyana and the other members of Suitland High's cheerleading squad from really letting their school spirit shine — the cheerleading uniforms.

To Tatyana and her crew, they were the worst of four-letter words — U-G-L-Y!

"The coaches were the ones giving us the uniforms. We would put them on, look at ourselves in the mirror, and say, *'Oh, no!'*"

That's when Tatyana jumped fast into action.

She turned *"Oh, no!"* into *"Let's go!"*

"I went home and sketched a few uniform designs — tops and bottoms that would show off our school colors in the best possible way. When I presented my ideas to my coaches and friends, they loved them. That's how my business started — with a simple need and a desire to make something that already existed even better."

Tatyana created what she calls a "flashy-hot" uniform featuring a top hat.

Her designs caught the attention of her competitors at cheerleading championships, and Just Cheer Uniforms was born.

Soon, Tatyana and her company had people *cheering for them*! Kids were on the sidelines calling out "F-L-A-S-H-Y H-O-T!" and wondering where they could get those uniforms with sparkle and class.

The uniforms cost $600 each, but this hasn't slowed the demand for them. "The hardest part is trying to explain my business's value, and why people will pay so much for the uniforms," Tatyana says.

But Tatyana knows her customer well. "There are cheerleading fans who are serious about this sport, which

means they'll pay anything for a quality and stylish uniform."

Tatyana not only designs and manages the manufacturing of cheerleading outfits and accessories, she is currently working on a special project with the Washington Redskins Cheerleaders — thanks in part to her involvement in the NFTE competition. (R-E-A-D on for more!)

Tatyana's prospectus captured first place at her high school business plan competition and at the Greater Washington, D.C., business plan competition.

But when it was time to face the judges at the NFTE national competition in New York City — and when she checked out the other competitors — Tatyana's confidence took a tumble. "I bit off my $42 French manicure," she remembers.

Once she started presenting her business plan, though, Tatyana was ready to S-C-O-R-E big. "I know my business, so there was really no question the judges could stump me with."

Tatyana was a solid player on game day. During a break in the competition, one of the judges offered to introduce her to the Washington Redskins Cheerleaders and to the head of marketing and promotion for the Redskins Cheerleading team.

Of course, Tatyana jumped at the chance. But even though this was her 50-yard-line ticket to becoming a cheerleading business champ, she kept her eyes on the NFTE competition prize, never losing sight of her goal in New York — to W-I-N!

CHEERS FOR TATYANA

TATYANA'S MOM, CELETA MCDOWNEY

"At nine years old, Tatyana told me she was going to be a millionaire, and I've never doubted it.

"I'm a mom who's always known her daughter would do something special with her spirited personality.  Tatyana can be rebellious at times. As a police officer, I'm all about limits and rules, and I'm not so thrilled when my daughter's rebellious streak shows itself.

"I try to remind Tatyana to use her defiance for good things. Rebelling against her school's cheerleading uniforms is what brought Just Cheer into being. Tatyana took a negative trait and turned it into something positive *and* profitable. I'm proud of that."

THE JUDGES ON TATYANA

Just Cheer is a solid business idea created from a real need. While many cheerleading uniform companies exist, Tatyana's is special because she has based her designs on what kids her age really want. She listens to her primary consumer — the teens who will be sporting Just Cheer uniforms to represent their school teams.

Some of us were ready to reach into our pockets and offer this girl money to take Just Cheer public. But there was one factor that made us stop — the cost of the uniforms. In today's economy, we wondered how many parents would be willing to spend $600 on a cheerleading uniform for their kids. When we asked Tatyana about this, she was ready with a strong response. She cited the durability and long-term value of her uniforms, and talked about how the uniforms would allow kids to invest in their futures. Undoubtedly, sports in its many varieties — including the uniforms, equipment, and promotional merchandise to go along with it — represents major business opportunities in the United States, so we were impressed. But not all of us were totally convinced. Time will tell if Just Cheer can make the grade.

STAND OUT IN A CROWD: HERE'S HOW

Whether you're designing sports uniforms or websites, the key to making an impression is getting noticed. Tatyana does this successfully through Just Cheer. Here are more ways to be a crowd-pleaser:

1. Go Day-Glo! Use bright colors in labels, stationery, and signs to attract people to your product.

2. In Vogue: Pay attention to what fashion forecasters say. If pink is the new black, incorporate it into your packaging.

3. Jingle. Create a catchy slogan that helps people remember your company's name. Try rhyming.

4. Sport It. If your product is wearable, show it off every chance you get. Make T-shirts or messenger bags that showcase your company's name, and ask friends and family members to serve as walking advertisements for you.

5. Pump Up the Glam! A little glitter goes a long way. Add sparkle whenever you can — if you can handle it!

6. Holiday Hip: Use special occasions and holidays to flaunt your stuff. For example, plan a special Fourth of July promotion around your product.

7. Borrow What Works. They say that imitation is the sincerest form of flattery, and that's true in business, too: So if you see an idea for, say, a used car lot that seems to be bringing in customers, adapt the concept for your company.

8. Mascot Fun: Sports teams use mascots to help promote themselves. Why not do the same thing? Is there a bulldog or bunny that can help sell your product?

9. Ya Gotta Luv Tchotchkes. Come up with an inexpensive and memorable giveaway that will keep your brand on people's minds. Key chains are one thing, but how about a sporty fabric cell phone cover you make yourself?

10. Expert Expertise: Bill yourself as a leading authority on your type of business, and volunteer to speak about it in public.

"GET OUT AND TALK TO DIFFERENT PEOPLE ABOUT YOUR BUSINESS IDEA. YOU HAVE TO GO AFTER IT; YOU CAN'T JUST WAIT FOR IT TO COME TO YOU."

sweet success

Jessica Cervantes

18

POPSY CAKES

Miami, Florida

Ever since her grandmother taught her how to bake, Jessica has loved measuring and tasting different ingredients, and experimenting with fun new flavors.

But it was not until Jessica enrolled in a business class at her high school that baking and business came together in a brand-new recipe for success.

For her business plan, Jessica created a new cupcake concept called Popsy Cakes — a cake on an edible cookie stick.

Jessica's family is from Cuba. They came to America to give Jessica the best life possible, and to offer her opportunities for a good education and future.

"My grandmother, who came to the United States in a small boat, is one of my biggest inspirations," Jessica says. *"Abuela* (Spanish for "grandmother") had a big sweet tooth. She taught me how to make millions of desserts from her homeland — everything from flan to *tres leches*. And when my father first arrived in Florida, he worked in a pizza place. So for me, baking has been everywhere."

Jessica's Popsy Cakes won first place in her high school's

business plan competition and second place in the South Florida regional competition.

The NFTE national competition put Jessica in a whole new league. She'd worked hard to get to New York, but now she really needed the right mix to take Popsy Cakes to a new level of sweet. In New York, the heat was on.

"I was shaking," she says. "And when it was time to present my business, I was stuttering because I was so nervous."

Thankfully, Jessica's mother came with her to help her stay focused and to coach her through the competition. "I'm such a perfectionist," says Jessica. "I want things to be so exact that sometimes people take it the wrong way — they think I'm being too stubborn."

The judges really challenged Jessica's exactness by asking her pointed questions about the economics and shelf-life of Popsy Cakes.

Jessica explained that each box of Popsy Cakes comes with twelve of the individually wrapped desserts. The box of twelve cakes makes one "unit."

She then outlined for the judges how much it costs to produce and package the cakes, and how much money her company earns on each unit after donating 5 percent of her profits to breast cancer research — sweet charity!

But Jessica's jitters got the best of her. "I got nervous, and wasn't clear on my numbers. First I said my cost per unit is $15, then quickly changed my answer to $12.75."

Jessica cited her net profit at $6,335.47. That means that

she takes home more than $6,000 each year after she spends money to make the cakes and have the boxes manufactured. But because of her uncertainty about unit costs, the judges weren't so sure.

One judge asked what happens if not all twelve cakes are eaten right away — what if a week goes by and there are cakes left over in the box?

Jessica was quick to answer. "The cakes last for more than two weeks, and are just as fresh as when they're first purchased."

The judges kept on with their questions. Had she thought of customizing the cakes? How can her customers offer feedback? What if someone buys a box of twelve cakes and loves chocolate, but not vanilla?

Jessica had already thought of that. Her website allows people to order online and send photos of designs, flavors, and colors they like.

Phew! That was the final question.

Afterward, Jessica took her seat and watched the other kids present their business plans. "I was so relieved when that part of the competition was over!" she says.

To congratulate her for a job well done and give her a bit of a sugar burst, Jessica's mom came quickly over to her daughter and offered her the best treat ever — a chocolate chip Popsy Cake. Her favorite flavor.

JESSICA'S PARENTS ARE SWEET ON THEIR DAUGHTER

JESSICA'S DAD, JORGE CERVANTES, AND JESSICA'S MOM, BARBARA ALVAREZ

"We've always been proud of Jessica. Some parents worry about their daughters and their futures, but we never worry about Jessica. She's got her head on straight and she's clear about where she's going. When Jessica came to us to tell us about her dream of starting a cake business, we just looked at each other and smiled. This was so Jessica! Before we even got the chance to ask her about her idea,  she pulled out a business plan and started explaining.

"To prepare for the competition, Jessica worked very hard. She spent months in our kitchen perfecting her Popsy Cakes after school, refining her business plan at night, and getting up early each morning to practice her presentation for the judges. Our home has become a Popsy Cakes factory — with Jessica leading the way."

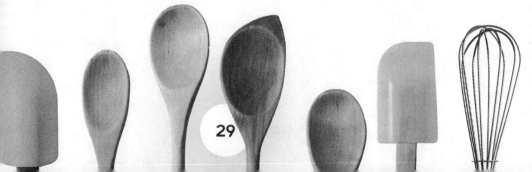

THE JUDGES ON JESSICA

This young lady's got a lot going for her. Popsy Cakes is an innovative idea that she's articulated very clearly. Jessica is passionate about her business and comes to this with one distinct competitive advantage — she has fully researched the market and knows where her product stands, who her audience is, and what makes her cakes unique.

There are many competitors for cakes, and we wondered what could be special about another dessert product. But Jessica came up with a twist on baked goods — the edible stick — that we thought was really remarkable.

Jessica presented Popsy Cakes well. She stuttered, which made her seem unsure about the cost of goods sold. Her profit appeared to be a lot less than what she outlined. This could hurt her in the long run.

She's a very polished presenter, but she talks very fast. It's important to speak clearly, slowly, and convincingly when presenting your business to others. Jessica could benefit from one simple tweak to her presentation — slowing it down a bit. She has so many valuable things to say about her business, and she needs to make sure each and every one of them is heard by listeners.

Given the miscalculation in numbers, we asked one another, "Can Popsy Cakes rise to the top?"

JESSICA'S TOP TEN TIPS FOR KEEPING THE FLAVOR IN A BUSINESS

1. Dream big! I believe there will be a Popsy Cakes boutique next to every Starbucks in the world.

2. Don't be afraid to make mistakes. Some of my best recipes came from happy accidents.

3. Research all aspects of your industry. For me, this means everything from frosting distributors to food coloring companies.

4. Keep an up-to-date calendar at all times. Great time management is important in business.

5. Be organized and clean — in and out of the kitchen.

6. Stay on top of your game by knowing your competitors. I go online every day to research new products that might resemble my Popsy Cakes. Then I make mine better!

7. Believe in what you say. People want to see someone who is assertive and in control. This will boost any presentation.

8. Network to meet new people. You'll be surprised how many connections you can make. Sometimes the most unlikely introduction can result in a business connection — even if they sell rubber and you sell cupcakes.

9. Ask others for their advice — especially leaders in the industry you're trying to break into. I send free samples to receive feedback.

10. My favorite equation: Promote + Advertise = Sales.

"HOW WOULD I DESCRIBE MYSELF? I AM A SCHOLAR." — RODNEY

"BUSINESS COMPETITIONS TEACH YOU MORE THAN JUST ENTREPRENEURSHIP — THEY TEACH YOU ABOUT REAL LIFE." — GABRIEL

co-ceos

18

Gabriel Echoles & Rodney Walker

18

FOREVER LIFE MUSIC & VIDEO PRODUCTIONS

Chicago, Illinois

Gabriel Echoles and Rodney Walker started out as casual classmates but quickly became close friends once they realized they had common interests. When Gabriel enrolled in an entrepreneurship class during their senior year at ACE Technical Charter High School in Chicago, his teacher suggested that he pair up with Rodney to combine their creativity and turn it into a business plan. That's how their company, Forever Life Music & Video Productions, got started.

Rodney came to the class with video production experience. Gabriel brought his love for singing, which he has been impressing people with since he was a little kid.

Music and videos, the two realized, were a classic combination — and not just on MTV or YouTube.

Forever Life Music & Video Productions makes customized digital videos with original music and songs, composed for special occasions.

Rodney and Gabriel, who call themselves "Co-CEOs," are in the business of making special memories last. When it's prom time and someone wants to capture that special night with the

music that made it memorable, Forever is there, bringing it all home. Same for birthday parties, weddings, family reunions, and other unforgettable events.

These young men bring a lot of heart to their business. That's because they've each overcome some hard obstacles, and they know the importance of holding on to good times.

When Rodney was five years old, he was placed in foster care with six of his nine brothers and sisters. And, for a brief time, he was even homeless. But there was one thing that kept Rodney going — the hope he had for a brighter future. When he took the business class at school, he learned that he had the power within himself to succeed.

Rodney's teacher, Michael McGrone, has been an important influence on Rodney. Mr. McGrone encouraged Rodney to stay in school, which he did.

Rodney's business has allowed him to dream big. "You have to visualize yourself and the way you want your life to be," Rodney says. "Thirty years from now, I'll be living in a big house. I'll have a nice, beautiful business. Most important, I'll be able to preserve the happiness I've been longing for all my life."

Gabriel, who is also from the South Side of Chicago, is the son of a mom who had him when she was 17 and was not able to care for him on her own. Gabriel has been raised primarily by Mary Walker, his grandmother, a very strong woman who's kept him focused on his goals. Thanks to his grandmother, Gabriel knows the importance of education, especially in launching and maintaining a company.

Forging a business as partners has shown Rodney and Gabriel the power of teamwork, and reminds both young men that when the going gets tough, a friend can help you make it through.

"The best part about working with Gabriel," says Rodney, "is that when I'm feeling frustrated, he can always lighten me up with his great sense of humor."

Gabriel returns the compliment, saying, "The best thing about working with Rodney is that he's reliable."

It was this winning combination of traits that helped Forever Life Music & Video Productions win first place in the Chicago citywide business plan competition. And it was a keen respect for teamwork that Rodney brought to New York for the NFTE national competition, where he represented the duo.

The two put many hours into polishing their business plan and presentation for the New York competition. "We spent every day together, and sometimes, without even talking, we understood each other," Gabriel says.

This connection was just what Rodney needed to stand up to the judges. When he got to New York, Rodney felt confident, but was held back by one thing. "Stage fright is the biggest fear I have in the world," he says.

It was Gabriel's humor that eased Rodney's mind. Before the competition, Gabriel lightened Rodney up with some good jokes.

At the national competition, Rodney stepped to the podium with his head held high. He started by giving the judges something to think about. He said, "I want to commence this presentation with a quote from Oscar Levant, a renowned pianist of the twentieth century who said, 'Happiness is not something you *experience*, it's something you *remember*.'"

This opening line impressed the judges, and made them listen closely as Rodney outlined his total cost of sales. He'd prepared a strategic plan for his company, and explained that he and Gabriel expected to produce 51 videos in the coming year, giving them a total net profit of $16,221.

The judges had a bunch of questions for Rodney.

Fifty-one videos is a lot for two guys to produce — just about one a week for the whole year. One judge wanted to know how Rodney and Gabriel would make sure each of their videos were produced with the best quality, given that they are the company's only employees. For Rodney, the answer was simple. "I told the judges that Gabriel and I would be building a management team."

When Rodney saw the judges smiling and nodding, he knew this was a great answer.

One judge pretended he was a customer who was about to get married. He told Rodney that his fiancée's favorite singer

was Alicia Keys, and that he wanted to incorporate Alicia Keys's music into their wedding video. The judge asked how Forever Life Music & Video Productions would handle this request.

"Easily," Rodney told him. Then Rodney outlined how customers can incorporate their favorite songs into their videos all by themselves if they want to.

Next came a question about marketing plans. Another easy one for Rodney, who, with Gabriel, had developed a "360 degree" approach to promotion that would get their message to customers in as many ways as possible and, like a playlist, would include several options for catering to customers' tastes and preferences.

More smiles from the judges.

Like his marketing plan, Rodney had come full circle — 360 degrees. His stage fright was gone, and he felt that for the moment he was home free.

When Rodney returned to his seat, the Co-CEO sat back to check out the next contestants and their presentations. The other young entrepreneurs sure knew their stuff. The competition was far from over. Watching and waiting seemed like *forever.*

RAVES FOR THE CO-CEOS FROM THEIR FAMILIES AND FRIENDS

RODNEY'S HIGH SCHOOL TEACHER, MICHAEL MCGRONE

"Rodney can't afford to fail. He's been to the bottom. I told Rodney, 'Be thankful for your struggles, because your struggles are going to prepare you for greatness.' And that's what's happened for this exceptional kid. He's turned his most troubling life experiences into opportunities."

RODNEY'S BROTHER, VINCENT WALKER

"Rodney's always known that to be a success in life, he had to have a good education. He's been like a 100-watt light in our family. We've cheered Rodney on at every phase of the competition, but we also applaud Rodney every day for being a Walker with purpose."

GABRIEL'S MOM, YOLANDA WALKER

"I'm so grateful for my son and for my own mother, who helped raise him. They say it takes a village to bring up a child, and Gabriel's got a community of people around him who believe in him and his future. My mother, Mary Walker, was always telling Gabriel to work hard in school, and he listened to this advice."

GABRIEL'S GRANDMOTHER, MARY WALKER

"I have one thing to say about Gabriel — he's definitely going to do well in college — and in everything he puts his mind to. Period."

THE JUDGES ON RODNEY

Time stopped when Rodney spoke. He's very articulate, poised, and polished. Here's a kid with a lot of confidence, but he's not cocky about it at all, which is key to being a business owner. Rodney and Gabriel had thought through the most important aspects of their company's growth — net profits, marketing, and customer satisfaction.

One intriguing aspect of Forever Life Music & Video Productions is the "mix-and-match" approach to customizing videos with music that the client chooses. We liked this, but it's a service that other video companies offer. We couldn't help but wonder, *What is truly unique about this business?* Special events video companies are everywhere. And technology is constantly changing and improving: These days, many "amateur directors" can create impressive personal films on their own computers, and then post them for the world to see on YouTube or social networking sites. In order to make Forever Life Music & Video Productions stand out, Gabriel and Rodney will need to develop a few more distinguishing features.

RODNEY'S TOP TEN TIPS FOR GETTING YOUR BUSINESS READY FOR A CLOSE-UP

1. Take initiative, then see it through. There are those with business plans, and there are those with businesses; the difference between the two is the labor.

2. Don't be afraid to fail. In almost all cases, success only comes after trying, failing a few times, and learning from your mistakes; and it feels that much more satisfying because it's been earned.

3. Accept criticism. Whether it's good or bad, criticism lets you know how customers and prospective investors really feel about your business. Develop a thick skin, and keep an open mind. Use all feedback to your advantage.

4. Follow up. When starting a business, opportunities leave you just as easily as they come. So return phone calls. Answer e-mails and text messages. Follow up on all requests and inquiries about your company.

5. There are a million ways to make a million dollars. Don't be discouraged if your original plan doesn't pan out as you'd expected. Success doesn't have a single pathway. Other avenues will always be available, it's just up to you to find them.

6. Think positive. Stay away from adversity. Focus on people who motivate, inspire, and encourage you to go forward.

7. Teamwork is a two-way street. For those who are considering partnerships, it is very important to share responsibilities, and hold both yourself and your partner accountable.

8. Do your research. No one should be able to tell you anything that you don't already know about your business.

9. Get tech-savvy. Keep up with the trends and technology that relate to your business. Technology can make your work process more efficient, and it can keep your product relevant. Be innovative. Discover ways to differentiate yourself from your competitors.

10. Stay balanced. Starting and operating a company can be very stressful. Remember to make time for the important things in life.

"PUT ALL YOU
HAVE INTO IT."

CHAPTER 4

TOUCH-DOWN TEEN

Macalee Harlis, Jr.

19

mac SHIELDS
Fort Lauderdale, Florida

For Mac Harlis, Jr., business is all about *not* seeing the light. When it came time to create a business plan for the entrepreneurship class he was taking in school, Mac was stumped for an idea — until he looked up at his teacher, who was wearing transition sunglasses. "It was like magic. As soon as I looked at my teacher, Mr. Rutledge, and stared closely at his sunglasses, I saw it — my business opportunity. It just hit me all of a sudden. I was like, 'that needs to be on a football shield.'"

Mac, a standout player on the Dillard High School football team, immediately thought about how hard it was to play football with the sun in your eyes, or camera lights flashing, or stadium lights changing from bright to brighter.

The answer was right under Mac's nose — or right in front of his eyes. He took the business ball and ran with it!

MAC Shields — football helmet shields tinted with special paint that transitions from clear to dark depending on the intensity of the light — was a great solution that got Mac a winning grade for his business class and won him prizes in local business contests.

To conceptualize his idea, Mac began by drawing sketches. He designed shields in many possible styles and with many different options to fit them onto football helmets. So that he could develop a shield that would be a cut above everyday

sunglasses, which are tinted a single shade to deflect the sun, Mac studied the technology of how transition lenses work.

The concept is simple: When a player uses a MAC Shield, the brighter it gets outside on the football field, the darker the shield gets. But, unlike traditional sunglasses, the MAC Shield darkens instantly and can withstand the shoves and slams football players face in every game.

Because Mac has spent many hours playing football with light blinding his view, he knows how important his shields are. And he's a kid who appreciates and *feels* the heat of competition. When his football team, who were district champions, lost second-round playoffs, it hit Mac hard. "I like to win. I'm always watching the guy on my left and the one on my right, checking out how they play the game. If you don't bring it, the other person will. That's why it's important to be my best. That's why I always bring it."

Mac named his company after himself and his father, Macalee Harlis, Sr. Mac credits his dad as his greatest influence and the source of his determination to succeed. "My dad expects a lot from me, because he knows I can do it."

Mac Sr. gave up the chance to attend college to support Mac Jr.'s grandmother, who was ill. He later become a custodian for the Fort Lauderdale school system.

Launching a company that bears his name made Mac even more determined to win the NFTE national competition. He wanted to do right by his name, and he wanted to make his dad even more proud.

In New York, Mac brought his A game, full-on. "When I woke

up that morning, I told myself to think of the NFTE competition like a football game. Nobody can beat me but me."

Mac had a lot riding on the competition. He had plans to attend Florida Atlantic University, and he knew that the contest prize money would make it possible for him to stay in college without worrying about how he would finance his company. "I have this great life ahead of me. It's a waste of time to do nothing with it."

Playing football in front of hundreds of people had given Mac the experience of performance under pressure. But this was a different kind of pressure. Unlike playing with a team, Mac was now on the field, playing solo. His biggest challenge was to explain the technology that makes his shields unique, and to get his point across in eight short minutes. The stopwatch was ticking.

The judges were not familiar with the polycarbonate sheets of plastic used to make the shields or how the paint applied to the shields adheres to them once put inside a UV screen printer. This was lots of scientific stuff. How would the average person understand Macalee's concept? And how would he get his point across to potential investors? Before Macalee was able to fully elaborate on his business, the presentation buzzer rang.

Macalee's time was up. He'd run out the clock. For now, it was game over.

Fortunately, Macalee wasn't blinded by the light of the day's intensity. He knew that everybody plays until someone is pronounced a winner.

MACALEE'S FANS TALK ABOUT THEIR FAVORITE PLAYER

MAC'S DAD, MACALEE HARLIS, SR.

"I've always told Mac not to follow others, but to be his own person, to be a leader, and to have his own mind. I explained to him that if he didn't want to grow up and work for someone else, he had to go to school to learn how he could create his own business. Mac gets this idea. He's a smart kid. A quick study."

MAC'S FOOTBALL TEAMMATE, KEVIN BASS

"The most challenging thing about playing football with Mac is that even when you're tired, he makes you keep working. That's why he makes such a good business owner. He's all about it, twenty-four-seven."

MAC'S UNCLE, TONY PORTER

"Mac's very competitive. He'll get upset if he doesn't win. But he doesn't let other kids intimidate him. He's got a solid inner core. Mac has taught me that if you want to win, you've got to persevere."

THE JUDGES ON MACALEE

Macalee's years on the football field have shaped him into a focused competitor. He knows what he wants and is ready to go for it. He's also very articulate about his company and the strategic value that his shields have.

Macalee needs to devise a way to simplify his presentation and his discussion of the shields. Potential investors will want to know how the shields work, but more important, why people will want to buy them. And they'll want to be able to understand quickly and easily what the product is. We encourage Macalee to come up with a ten-word sound bite that explains the shields.

His business idea is one we hadn't seen before, and that set Macalee apart. But, among ourselves, we questioned the demand for a product such as the MAC Shield.

If Macalee were able to get an exclusive contract with a major football league such as the NFL, he'd have a solid chance of making it big. We also encourage him to register a trademark for his company's name and product. Doing so will help protect him from other businesses that, knowingly or not, might try to develop the same idea.

MACALEE'S GAME PLAN FOR SCORING BIG

1. Never say never. Others may tell you you'll never make it. Don't believe them.

2. The most successful entrepreneurs have fallen a time or two. Don't get frustrated when you fail — embrace setbacks, and keep moving forward!

3. Play your best game. While it's always a good idea to know what the competition is doing, use your own self-progress as a benchmark. Is your business earning more than it did a year ago? Has your customer base grown by a certain percentage?

4. Take a deep breath. Whether you're competing in a game or presenting to potential investors, a few deep breaths will calm you down and keep you focused.

5. Be passionate. You've got to love the game whether it's chess, football, or business. Whenever you talk about your business, let everyone know it's something you love doing.

6. Make it visual: When presenting your business plan, be sure to use words that paint pictures of your product for your audience. And bring visuals, too: a prototype of your product or a computer presentation.

7. Find out whether there's really a need for your product, and if similar products already exist. If there are others out there like yours, get information on how they've succeeded — or why they may have failed.

8. Always have a Plan B. It's rare that everything goes exactly as you expect, and you have to be ready to change your game to adapt to new situations.

9. Scan the playing field, 360 degrees. Don't focus too much on one or two aspects of your company while overlooking others. Organize your time so that you can give attention to all parts of your business; otherwise you just might get sideswiped or tackled from behind by an opponent you never even saw coming.

10. Have fun! School, sports, business: In a way, everything's just a game. Sometimes you win, sometimes you lose, and you can always play again. So never become too stressed over your business. Tension makes you lose sight of why you've become an entrepreneur.

"IF YOU DON'T TAKE RISKS, YOU'LL NEVER KNOW WHAT YOU COULD HAVE DONE."

PRETTY PACKAGING TAKES THE CAKE.

EVERYTHING'S COMING UP POPSY CAKES! JESSICA
CERVANTES CELEBRATES HER SWEET SUCCESS.

CHAPTER 5

TAKING CHARGE

Shan Shan Huang

19

CHARGER STATION
Boston, Massachusetts

Three years ago, Shan Shan was a high school student in southern China when her parents made a decision that would change the lives of their family forever. They immigrated to the United States to give their daughters a chance to get a first-rate education and to have a better quality of life. "This was so hard for my parents, but they knew America's education is good, so they gave up everything they had for us."

In China, Shan Shan never had the opportunity to learn about starting a business, so she jumped at the chance to take an entrepreneurship course at Charlestown High School.

For her business, Shan Shan designed a plan to import Chinese cell phone charger vending machines that she noticed in the airports and hotels in China. With so many people — especially teens — using cell phones, Shan Shan knew her idea had the right spark. One of the coolest aspects of the chargers she imports is that they can power up a cell phone in three minutes.

Sadly, Shan Shan's father passed away before she launched her company, but her dad's outgoing personality

is something Shan Shan takes with her wherever *she* goes, especially into competitions. She also has the continuing support of her mom, Feng He Mai, and her twin sister, Juan, who are always at Shan Shan's side, accompanying her every step of the way on this exciting journey to business ownership.

"My mom wanted me to be a pharmacist because she thinks it's a very comfortable, secure job," says Shan Shan. "But I want a bigger challenge. I want to be a successful businesswoman."

Shan Shan's initiative and charm, which she got from her father, and the guidance of her mom and sister, helped her take first place in the New England regional business plan competition.

In addition to learning how to build a business plan, Shan Shan has had to learn to speak English well enough to talk about her business to others. Imagine what a challenge that would be! But she studied hard, and now, only a few short years since she came to the United States, she speaks very well, and is confident in her abilities. And Shan Shan's passion for her venture translates easily. There is no language barrier holding back the excitement this young lady has for her company.

In New York, Shan Shan was super-ready to meet the judges. Before she even walked into the room with the other contestants, she quietly asked her dad to help her, to give her energy so that she could win. And she called upon the lessons her mom had taught her about saving money and

planning for the future. These qualities were at the core of the plan she would present to the judges.

Since the financial success of any company is all about the bottom line, Shan Shan got right to the fiscal aspects of her business. The screen behind her lit up and *bam!* Shan Shan showed off an income statement that was detail done right.

She came out strong, articulating the price per unit for each charger, and clearly outlined her company's return on investment. The judges' questions about money were no match for this math-savvy teen. She knew her numbers.

But the eight-minute clock was ticking, and Shan Shan was eager to talk to the judges about her discussions with Chinese manufacturers to adapt the cell phone charger devices for the American market.

This was one of those moments when talking fast helped. She got her message across just in time, and left the podium feeling as charged up and high-powered as one of her cell phones.

Back at her seat, Shan Shan whispered, *"Thank you, Dad."*

SHAN SHAN'S FAMILY & FRIENDS ARE PLUGGED IN TO HER SUCCESS

SHAN SHAN'S NFTE ADVISER, JESSICA ANGELL

"Shan Shan has this very polite and sweet side, and then, all of a sudden, she gets in front of an audience, and it's like watching an amazing performer. I didn't realize all of the sophistication that went into building Shan Shan's business plan, but I'm not surprised that she's been able to execute it all so well."

SHAN SHAN'S SISTER, JUAN

"I felt more nervous than Shan Shan. The whole time I was thinking, *Oh, Daddy, please let her win.*"

SHAN SHAN'S MOM, FENG HE MAI

"Shan Shan is very lovely and endearing, but that has never

stopped her. I can't speak English fully, and this has prevented me from getting a good job in America. I'm so proud of both my daughters, who have learned the language well enough to make their voices heard. When I look at Shan Shan and all that she's accomplished, my heart sings."

THE JUDGES ON SHAN SHAN

Here is a young lady who knows her stuff. For any business to be fiscally sound — to be profitable — it needs to have a solid financial plan. We were immediately struck with the control Shan Shan had over her numbers.

Advances in technology are happening very quickly all over the world. To keep her business on the cutting edge, Shan Shan will have to stay on top of the rapid changes happening in this arena.

Being from China and having the ability to speak both Cantonese and English fluently is an advantage for Shan Shan. Because of China's leadership in our technological age, Shan Shan is poised to take her business to global heights.

There is also a sizable population who can benefit from her cell phone chargers. How many of us have had a cell phone run out of juice and have had to wait until we're back home to recharge? Shan Shan's product buys its users one of the most sought-after commodities of the modern age — time. And since time is money, many people will be eager to get what Shan Shan has to offer.

SHAN SHAN'S TOP TEN TIPS FOR MAKING BUSINESS CONNECTIONS

1. Service, service, service. Remember, you're giving to your customers. They come first. Always provide top-notch service to keep people coming back.

2. Talk to your customers — and encourage them to talk to you. Look for ways to solicit customer feedback, such as by blogging or posting comments on your company's website. When the feedback comes, pay attention.

3. Reward customer loyalty: Make them feel good about purchasing your product. Offer incentives — like discounts or bonus minutes.

4. Expand your point-of-view. Look for ways to see your business in a different light. For example, if you're mainly targeting teens, also consider the needs of senior citizens, stay-at-home moms, working parents, and how they, too, can benefit from your product.

5. Study hard. Think of your company as something you're always learning more about. Read up on your industry. Follow trade publications and websites. Attend free seminars if you get the chance. Ask questions.

6. Build relationships. Share information about your business with everyone you meet. This is how connections are made. Spread news about your company to your teachers, classmates, coworkers, family, and friends.

7. Say good-bye to shy. To be an effective business owner, you can't be a wallflower. Be assertive. Speak up! If you really suffer from shyness, take a class in public speaking.

8. Plan. It's like the saying goes: If you fail to plan, you plan to fail. The best way to succeed is to put a road map in place before starting your business. The best blueprint is a solid business plan.

9. Don't waste your time or your money. Always look for good values when purchasing supplies and equipment for your business. Then pass these smart savings on to your customers by offering competitive prices.

10. Those who take risks often take home prizes. Be a risk-taker.

"STARTING MY OWN
BUSINESS HAS TAUGHT ME
THAT IF YOU WANT TO DO
SOMETHING, YOU SHOULD
NEVER LET ANYONE TELL
YOU YOU CAN'T."

CHAPTER 6

PUPPY LOVE

Amanda Loyola

15

ECODOG TREATS LLC
New York, New York

A broken heart was the start of a business for Amanda.

After her dog, Princess, died of cancer, Amanda put her grief into something positive: helping other dogs live long, healthy lives. Right away, she began to research the ingredients in pet food, and found out that red meat, which contains chemicals from cattle feed, was one of the leading causes of cancer in dogs.

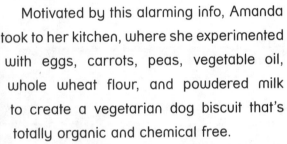

Motivated by this alarming info, Amanda took to her kitchen, where she experimented with eggs, carrots, peas, vegetable oil, whole wheat flour, and powdered milk to create a vegetarian dog biscuit that's totally organic and chemical free.

She added brown sugar, baked the treats into heart-shaped goodies, and, as a final touch, sprinkled in the love she still has for Princess.

And oh, did that love go a long way! She named her doggie snacks EcoDog Treats, and hit the streets of New York City to test them out on the hungriest hounds and the pickiest poodles in the 'hood.

Amanda set her biscuits down onto the sidewalk next to a leading grilled meat dog food, and the pooches came running! They were quick to reject the riblets, and gobbled up her EcoDog offerings faster than a beagle takes to a bone.

The proof was right there on the pavement, and dogs don't lie! Amanda knew she was onto something awesome.

Others were quick to see it, too. Amanda took first place in the New York Metro regional business plan competition.

Entrepreneurship, new ventures, and cooking are all part of Amanda's family heritage.

Amanda's father, Cesar, grew up in a *favela* (a Portuguese word that means "slum") of Rio de Janeiro, Brazil, and came to America. With his limited English, he began working at the local Burger King in Manhattan, but later launched his own business as a personal chef. He taught Amanda everything he knows about starting a company from scratch and whipping up the right ingredients to make it succeed.

Amanda's mom, Iona, is the family visionary. She's always been the one to inspire Amanda and her father to dream big. "I use my parents as examples of how to live a good life. They came to America with nothing, and they've made it."

Amanda is thankful to have such strong and loving parents and for their hard work and ingenuity — traits she's happy to have inherited. "I think the American Dream is a lot more than just money," she says. "We're not the wealthiest family, but we're one of the happiest. To me, that's part of the American Dream."

Since the NFTE competition was right in Amanda's hometown, she eased into the competition without the stress of traveling to a new city. But city smarts didn't help with how nervous Amanda was when she saw the judges and the other kids in the contest. Her mom was nervous, too. "My heart was pounding," she said. "I was like, *Oh my God, oh my God, oh my God!*"

In her presentation, Amanda talked about her motivations

for starting her company and told the judges about Princess. She described EcoDog Treats as more than just a business that makes dog food. "I explained to the judges that I'm the CEO of a manufacturing and retail company so that they would see the scope of my venture."

Like the other contestants, Amanda outlined her business plan, which covered most of the key aspects of her company.

Then the hard questions started. One of the first things the judges wanted to know about was shelf space. With any product, there is a cost to stock items on the shelves of stores. This had not been factored into Amanda's calculations. The judges asked if Amanda had even considered this.

Ruh-roh! She hadn't.

The best answer she could give was to tell the judges she'd look into shelf space costs. But being unprepared didn't look good for Amanda, and she knew it. She recovered quickly when one of the judges asked her what she'd learned by studying economics in school. "I told him about supply and demand, and perceived value. You can't price your product too low, or the demand for it decreases because people don't think it's as valuable."

This answer seemed to win back the judges. Feeling more confident, Amanda continued by explaining the structure of her business.

EcoDog Treats is an LLC — a limited liability company. This allows Amanda to retain full ownership of her venture.

Amanda hoped that the intent behind her business, the results of her canine taste tests, and her LLC status would be enough to convince the judges of her company's potential.

AMANDA'S PARENTS SPEAK FROM THE HEART

CESAR LOYOLA, AMANDA'S DAD, AND IONA LOYOLA, AMANDA'S MOM

"Amanda is our only child. We feel blessed to have such a terrific daughter. It was always our dream to come to America, and Amanda has made this dream-come-true so incredibly special. When she lost her dog, Princess, she took it very hard. It was such a sad thing for a teenager to go through. Amanda's always been strong, but we worried and wondered how she would handle the loss of her beloved pet. It's been great to watch her turn a tragedy into something meaningful and helpful to others.

"Talking about Amanda is hard at times — because we can't help but brag about her. We've always been a close family, but this whole experience has brought us even closer.

"We're lucky to have such a terrific teenager. She can be hardheaded. She likes things her way. But that's how we are, too — stubborn and a little too intense at times. We know Amanda will take the best of these qualities — such as turning stubbornness into tenacity — and make them work for her as she builds her business."

THE JUDGES ON AMANDA

This is a young lady with a lot of personal and professional integrity. She cares about people, the environment, and pets. Dogs are one of the most popular pets in America, and in many countries throughout the world. And with the increasing emphasis on healthy, environmentally friendly products for pets, Amanda's got a good chance of making her business into something that's not only meaningful, but profitable.

Amanda hadn't considered the expense involved in stocking items on store shelves. This was a costly oversight in her presentation. Shelf space is something every business owner who intends to sell products through retail means must consider.

We were most impressed with Amanda's foresight in structuring her business. A limited liability company (LLC) allows her to maintain complete control of her company's quality, growth, and future. When a business is founded on important personal values, as Amanda's is, the LLC status gives the owner the power to make sure those values are maintained even as her company grows.

AMANDA'S TOP TEN TIPS FOR PUTTING THE BARK IN YOUR BUSINESS

1. Know who your customers are. Who needs your product most? If no one needs what you have to offer, you can't be successful.

2. Get professional help. Seeking advice from experts in your field (in my case, veterinarians) is really important for creating a successful, efficient, and useful company.

3. Plan your finances. Get funding before you start and create a business plan to keep yourself on track.

4. Go green. By focusing your business goals on keeping the environment safe, you're helping to build a healthier world and a brighter future for everyone.

5. Lock in legal issues. Find a lawyer who can advise you on getting legal approvals and any necessary licenses cleared before you launch your business.

6. Test the waters — or the streets. Market research is best done with those who will actually use your product. By offering taste tests or letting people (or pets) try your product, you're gaining valuable information, even if it's expressed in a wagging tail or a happy bark!

7. Details before sales. Entrepreneurs who can account for all costs of their product provide potential investors with the assurance that their money will be wisely spent.

8. Heed the P's — be professional and prepared. Dress like a business owner. First impressions mean a lot.

9. Work hard. Being a slacker never got anyone ahead.

10. Stay flexible. Consumer needs are always changing. Adjust yourself to those needs so that you can meet them.

"WE'VE LEARNED THAT
TO BE IN BUSINESS YOU
HAVE TO TAKE RISKS."
— WILLIAM

"GOOD THINGS CAN
COME FROM JUMPING
INTO THE UNKNOWN."
— JA'MAL

smooth OPERaTORS

16

William Mack & Ja'Mal Wills

17

J&W sensations
Baltimore, Maryland

Even though William and Ja'Mal own a business that's all about being soft, they've worked hard to build their venture. Their business, J&W Sensations, makes moisturizers that rejuvenate and soften the skin.

The idea for their company grew out of a school science class at Patterson High. While other kids were filling test tubes and beakers with bubbly chemicals and acidic compounds, Ja'Mal and William were reading product labels and learning about the high number of chemicals in typical body lotions.

They were in science class to learn, not to impress the

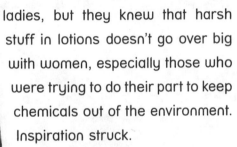

ladies, but they knew that harsh stuff in lotions doesn't go over big with women, especially those who were trying to do their part to keep chemicals out of the environment. Inspiration struck.

Out came their science lab safety goggles — and their ingenuity. Like the other kids in class, they began mixing and experimenting, but their concoctions were far from explosive. They started with some cucumbers, threw in a few melon chunks, added herbs, and whipped it all together in a soda bottle.

No, this was not a new smoothie recipe or a tropical dessert topping. And at first, it came out all wrong. Even

after several tries at shaking and stirring, the potion was not happening. It was too watery. Then too sticky. Then too *icky*.

Just as the guys were about to kiss their brew good-bye, they whipped it up just right, and their product was ready to sell. It was a line of organic, chemical-free lotions that make skin soft as a peach.

They shared their invention with anyone eager to take the ash off their elbows and knees, or who just wanted smoother skin. But they kept their recipe under wraps. After all, a true entrepreneur never reveals *all* of his secrets. The two friends knew they had lotions that weren't like any other, and they were ready to make their business happen.

It didn't take long for the good news to spread. "Our instincts were right," William says. "Girls love our cucumber-melon lotion."

"And they appreciate that our lotions are all-natural," says Ja'Mal.

The J&W Sensations business plan took first place in the Baltimore citywide business plan competition.

But that was just the beginning for these entrepreneurs. They knew that to get to the nationals — and to win — they'd have to go back to the beakers and the drawing board to test and perfect their lotion formulas, which they did. During summer break after their junior year in high school, while most kids were staying cool by licking ice cream, these business partners were burning with creativity — and making *skin* creams.

They were also crunching numbers to iron out the wrinkles in their business plan.

"The best thing about working with Ja'Mal is that I can always trust him," says William. "The *worst* thing was finalizing our business plan. Ja'Mal is cool, but he's got a mind of his own. I would ask Ja'Mal to do one thing, and he'd do another."

The days leading up to the national competition were stressful. "We started getting on each other's nerves," Ja'Mal remembers. "But then we just said, 'Hey, we're business partners. We've got to stick together!'"

By the time they arrived in New York for the national competition, the two were smooth.

They presented their plan together, kicking off with cucumber-melon as their premier product.

The first thing the judges asked about was their competition. How, they wondered, would J&W stand up to big-name distributors like Bath & Body Works and Johnson & Johnson?

This was a question Ja'Mal and William had practice fielding from before they'd even won the Baltimore competition. It seemed everyone wanted to know the answer. So by the time they'd made it to the nationals in New York, the boys had a well-planned response at the ready. To their way of

thinking, they had two key competitive advantages. According to their market research, the average product price at Bath & Body Works was about $9.50. For Johnson & Johnson, $5.59. The average price for J&W lotions is $8.00. Though Johnson & Johnson products are less expensive, they are marketed mostly as lotions for babies. J&W lotions are for everyone.

Also, through testing, the boys had confirmed that J&W Sensations are effective for most types of skin. Other lotion products, even those that claimed to be "all-natural," could sometimes irritate sensitive skin. J&W had a track record for soothing most kinds of skin. From the boys' point of view, this both broadened the potential market and justified the price of their products.

Ja'Mal and William also had a plan for possibly turning their competitors into friends, and leveraging the assets of the name-brand companies. "We'd thought of approaching Johnson & Johnson as a potential sponsor for our product line," William says. This impressed the judges. It showed that the boys were thinking big — the hallmark of ambitious businesspeople.

THE SMOOTH TRUTH ON WILLIAM MACK AND JA'MAL WILLS

THE PRINCIPAL OF PATTERSON HIGH SCHOOL, LAURA LEE D'ANNA

"These kids work so well together, which is key for business partners. They have excellent timing when they're presenting themselves. They can finish each other's sentences. Ja'Mal and William are the pride of our school. The very fact that they won a local NFTE business competition — that's a first for Patterson."

THEIR TEACHER, ROBERT BROWN

"William and Ja'Mal are good students, but they do act up every once in a while. They like to have fun, which inspires others — in a good way."

WILLIAM'S MOM, EDNA MACK

"It's a miracle to see my son do what he does. I'm so proud of him."

JA'MAL'S DAD, ANDRE WILLS

"My son and his friend have a lot of ambition. They'll be bigger than Johnson & Johnson!"

THE JUDGES ON WILLIAM & JA'MAL

These two are a good reminder that being in business is about having fun and doing what you love. That's sure true of these guys. They made all of us smile with their sincerity and humor about the virtues of fruity organic lotions and how appealing they are to eco-conscious women.

But this team is not all fun and games. They know their stuff. By studying the competition, they've gained an accurate picture of where they stand on the competitive landscape and how their products fit in.

It's smart of them, too, to consider ways larger companies can help them. Small businesses often seek out industry leaders for merger opportunities. If J&W were to secure a line of lotions within the product family of a well-known cosmetics manufacturer, they would have the opportunity to reach a larger customer base through wider distribution. There's a drawback to this tactic, though. Once you join forces with the big guys, you lose total control of your company.

Finally, we asked ourselves — how special are these lotions, really? The market for such products is very saturated now. To get ahead, J&W Sensations will need to offer something consumers can get nowhere else.

WILLIAM & JA'MAL'S
TOP TEN TIPS FOR
KEEPING SLICK

1. Think short term and long term. Develop plans for one year, five years, ten years, twenty. Twelve-month goals help you reach twelve-year goals. Plan wisely, and update your plan often.

2. The right handshake and smile go a mile. When meeting someone, give a firm handshake and warm smile. Nobody likes a limp fish and a frown.

3. Business cards and logos should reflect who you are — and they should be memorable.

4. Do what you love. Launch a business that is fun for you.

5. Supply and demand are key business concepts. Understand these and you'll be able to control your costs, sales, and inventory.

6. Aim to always have a ready answer for any question someone asks you about your business. And if you're ever caught on the spot, speechless, first thank that person for bringing the oversight to your attention — then find out the answer and get back to them ASAP.

7. Find a mentor. If you meet someone who has the success you want, ask them how they've achieved it and if they can guide you in your goals. Stay in touch with that person. Let them know about your triumphs and ask for help with setbacks.

8. Talk the talk — walk the walk. If you want people to take you seriously, speak articulately about your company, but also conduct yourself like a business owner. And always follow through.

9. Stay fresh. Constantly come up with new ideas to keep the customers lining up.

10. Easy does it. Business ownership can be stressful. Clear your head when pressures mount. If you're in business with a partner, take time out to laugh and to acknowledge your successes so far. You'll remember why you decided to team up in the first place!

"ALWAYS THINK
POSITIVE, POSITIVE,
POSITIVE."

CHAPTER 8

SIGN OF THE TIMES

Robbie Martin

17

THE DEAF ACADEMY
New Bedford, Massachusetts

If you blink, you might miss what Robbie Martin has to say. So keep your eye on Robbie. He's got something important to tell you.

Robbie, who has been deaf since birth, uses American Sign Language to communicate. When he was a baby, Robbie's parents were told by doctors that he would probably never sit or walk, and that he certainly would never be able to hear. Robbie's mom and dad refused to accept this. "My parents had a strong faith, and they knew this would see them through," says Robbie.

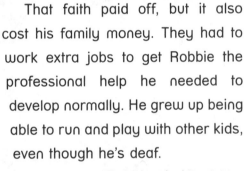

That faith paid off, but it also cost his family money. They had to work extra jobs to get Robbie the professional help he needed to develop normally. He grew up being able to run and play with other kids, even though he's deaf.

As a teen, Robbie tried to get an after-school job to help contribute to the family expenses. "Many times I applied for openings, but was turned down when they found out I was deaf. I gave my mother big headaches about money because I didn't have a job."

Knowing how much his parents had sacrificed to help his development when he was younger made Robbie even more determined to succeed. He was committed to someday helping his mother by earning money of his own.

Robbie hasn't let his lack of hearing slow him down. His message is all in his hands, and he knows well how to get his point across.

When his classmates at New Bedford High School started asking Robbie for sign language lessons, he taught them to sign during free periods, at lunch, and after school. He was happy to show them how, through a few simple signs, you can say important things. The other kids loved that when a teacher told them to "talk amongst yourselves," they could have a conversation without speaking. Sign language was like a secret code that could be cracked only by those who knew it.

Anyone who watches Robbie sign can see how cool it is to have all the answers at your fingertips. While teaching basic signing skills to children at the Kids College at Bristol Community College, which has several campuses in Massachusetts, Robbie saw an opportunity to combine his teaching ability and the need for his services. He created his business, The Deaf Academy, through his high school's entrepreneurship curriculum.

The concept is simple, but speaks volumes for how many ways people can communicate. Robbie placed third at the New England regional business plan competition.

When he got to the regional NFTE competition, he knew his biggest challenge would be to capture and then keep the attention of his audience. To cover the bases, Robbie brought along a sign language interpreter who spoke out loud while Robbie signed his presentation. But the interpreter's job was done almost as soon as Robbie stepped to the presentation

podium. After just a few moments, Robbie turned to his inter-preter and signed, "Voice off," which meant "stop talking."

That's when Robbie's sign language skills — and his business smarts — came into play. Through signing, he asked the judges if they wanted free tickets to the Celtics basketball game. None of them understood sign language, so they didn't answer.

Robbie's interpreter couldn't help but speak up on Robbie's behalf. "I asked the judges, 'Does anybody know what I just said?'"

The judges shook their heads.

Through his interpreter, Robbie told them, "You don't want to miss an opportunity like that again. If you took my class, that wouldn't happen."

Opportunity indeed! Robbie definitely had the judges' full attention now. And from then on, while Robbie's interpreter articulated his business plan, Robbie showed everyone how powerful sign language is. The entire room listened — and watched Robbie. This gave him a distinct advantage. All eyes were on him while he presented the details of his company. "I selected this business because I think people are really interested in learning sign language," Robbie explained.

Robbie has proof of that from his experience teaching kids across Massachusetts. And, thanks to the profits his Deaf Academy has earned, Robbie says, "Now I have my own money."

Robbie's business is a service endeavor, but the judges were quick to see that it was bringing in cash as well as making a difference.

THAT'S HER BOY

ROBBIE'S MOM, JEANNE MARTIN

"I always knew Robbie was going to have a business sense. That boy used to hoard his birthday money! He wanted to start a business to help out with the finances in the house.

I never asked Robbie for money, of course. I'm his mom, and I love him, and I would do whatever it took to help him. I didn't expect for him to pay for the doctors and specialists he's needed. But while growing up, Robbie was always there saying, 'I want to work! I want to work!'

"He's got a brilliant mind and I want him to be able to use it, which he's doing. At the NFTE competition, when Robbie told his interpreter to stop talking, I was freaking out! I was like, *What is he doing?!* And I was thinking, *Oh my goodness — he's losing their attention!*

"But when he came out with the Celtics joke, I was in my seat saying, 'That's my boy!'"

THE JUDGES ON ROBBIE

Watching Robbie's presentation showed us that we need to stretch ourselves. It's important to remember that business is all about effective interpersonal skills and being able to communicate with all kinds of people. Robbie's opening line was great.

We all could have gone to the Celtics game, but missed the chance because of our limited ability to understand an offer that had been presented to us. That made us ask a question of ourselves: Are we limited in our thinking?

With the increasing desire among educators and schools to welcome all kinds of kids into their classrooms and to create a diverse learning environment, more are seeking ways to serve special-needs students.

The same is true for parents who, like Robbie's, want to see their kids grow up and thrive in "mainstream" settings. So they're always looking for ways to help their children.

There aren't enough learning programs for deaf people and for others who want to be able to communicate through the use of sign language. Robbie has demand on his side — people want what he's offering.

One of the beautiful things about American Sign Language is that it's widely used. Robbie has the potential to make his business an accessible endeavor. He'll need to think carefully about staffing and hiring the best men and women who can teach sign language. A company's reputation is everything, especially when it involves working with young customers.

HEED THE NEED

Robbie's smarts make it clear that being deaf doesn't stop the show. Through his example, we see that people with special needs can always use the helping hand of someone who cares. If you've been touched in some way by a special-needs family member or friend, or if you simply want to better understand disabilities, here are ways to do it.

1. Raise your hand. Look for volunteer opportunities through schools, religious institutions, hospitals, and day-care centers.

2. Learn by doing. Find out how to meet the needs of the people you're seeking to help. Take a class in autism awareness or Braille.

3. Experience is the best teacher. Look for places that offer workshops on the actual experience of what it feels like to be dyslexic or physically challenged. Put yourself in someone else's shoes and walk their walk. Or spend a day in a wheelchair to see how it feels.

4. Slow it down. Sometimes kids with unique abilities need extra time to communicate or adjust to a new situation. Be patient.

5. Go out of your way. Lots of people have trouble making friends. But it can be harder for girls and boys who are different. When you encounter an individual whose needs and conditions are not like yours, reach out to that person. Show them you care.

6. Ask your teacher, doctor, or clergyperson if they know someone who may need a smiling face or a gentle word of encouragement.

7. Find common ground. We all have things that make us unique. But there are many things, too, that draw us together.

8. Pocket your pride. Some ignorant people may tell you it's not cool to hang out with those who struggle with disabilities. Who cares what they think? Do the right thing.

9. Get the facts. Misconceptions keep us ignorant, too. Read up on various disabilities to find out the real deal.

10. Visit your local library and check out books that highlight aspects of different experiences with disabilities. Ask your librarian for recommendations.

"BELIEVE IN YOURSELF,
AND YOU'LL DO IT. IF
YOU THINK NEGATIVE,
THEN IT'S NEVER
GOING TO HAPPEN."

an ax
TO GRIND

Alexander Niles

16

niles custom GUITarS
Miami, Florida

ude, here's a rocker who knows what he wants and will tell it to you straight: "I'm going to capture 10 percent of the world's custom electric guitar market."

To Alex Niles, this is not a dream — it's a plan. A plan he's been putting into play ever since he was old enough to know the name of rock legend Pete Townshend. "Sometimes I can be a bit overconfident," Alex says. But it's his self-assurance that has taken Alex far on the road to business ownership.

Alex, who is the son of immigrants — his dad is from Hungary, his mom from Uruguay — builds custom guitars. He blends craftsmanship, sound quality, and funky colors like intergalactic blue to make beautiful music — and a cool company called Niles Custom Shop Guitars.

As a kid, Alex's dad tried to get him to play baseball, but all he wanted to play was music. When his parents took him to the beach — a regular pastime in Miami — they brought a little ukulele for Alex to strum, and he loved it.

Alex never dreamed he could create a business from his passion — until he took an entrepreneurship class at Highland

Oaks Middle School. When his business plan won first place in the South Florida regional business plan competition, Alex used his prize money to create a custom guitar.

Alex got the idea from one of his favorite rock musicians. "Jimi Hendrix made his own guitar, so I thought I would make one, too."

Like Jimi, Alex has touched lots of listeners with the hard, sweet charge of his guitars' sounds. But making a custom instrument from scratch isn't cheap. To get his business started, Alex needed cash. He called on his favorite uncle, Milton Garcia, and asked for help.

Uncle Milton gave Alex $5,000 to start his company. When he handed over the money, he was clear with his nephew: This was not a loan. Alex's uncle told him he was an investor in his company. The gift was given with love because Uncle Milton believed in Alex, but Alex knew he had to show his uncle that the money would be well spent.

Alex made a promise. He told Uncle Milton he would see a return on his investment within the first year of launching his company.

Then Alex strummed into fast action.

To distinguish his guitars from others, Alex knew they had to be superior instruments. He spent months crafting, perfecting, playing — working hard to get his guitars just right. He devised a guitar made of the highest-quality components, which he says is superior to Fenders and Gibsons, leading guitar brands.

In the music world, celebrity endorsements bring fans to

a product or service. In the same way that car companies and high-end watch manufacturers get models and movie stars to talk about their products on TV and pose with them in magazines, Alex got legendary Argentinean-born musician Alex Fox to star in a video clip on which he talks about the awesome appeal of Niles Custom Guitars. Fox is known for his hot Latin guitarsmanship. This was the perfect way to spice up the Niles marketing campaign. ¡Muy caliente!

That's showbiz, baby, and that's how Alex won over the judges.

He told them about his 10 percent market share plan, talked about the high quality of his guitars, and gave the judges a profile of his primary customer — hardcore musicians like himself who are serious about making good music.

"And in conclusion I'd like to play a few choice licks for you on my Niles Custom Guitar," Alex announced.

With this, Alex had them. The judges were rocking and feeling the music. Alex ended with a Pete Townshend leap, then landed in a split! (Unlike the legendary Who front man, though, there was no way Alex was going to smash his custom guitar to pieces on the stage!)

The judges were like, *Whoa, this kid means business.*

ALEX'S FANS ROCK THE HOUSE

ALEX'S TEACHER, STEVE COLYER

"When he did that kick-butt riff at the end of his presentation, I wasn't surprised. Alex is a true entertainer."

ALEX'S MOM, ANABEL NILES

"Watching Alex at the competition was like nothing I've ever seen. When he performed, I jumped out of my chair. It was unbelievable — but also totally Alex.

"Our son has always been ambitious. Even as a teenager, he's a bit of a workaholic, which I think he gets from me and his dad. His big weakness is that he needs to listen more. Like every kid, he doesn't like to do what his mother tells him. But this is why he makes a great entrepreneur — he's an independent thinker."

ALEX'S DAD, JIM NILES

"Alex is a true perfectionist. I've tried to talk to him about running his business. Sometimes he listens; sometimes not. I've told him that the structure of his business will change when he starts to hire employees. But he just shakes his head like he knows already. Alex seems to have a master plan, and I'm not going to mess with it."

ALEX'S UNCLE, MILTON GARCIA

"Alex is a kid who loves to create. Working hard is in his blood — so is stubbornness. If someone tells him to do something he doesn't like, he won't do it.

"It's been very special for me watching Alex grow his company. The best part for me was when Alex called and said, 'Uncle Milton, I want you to be with me in my project.' All I could say was, 'Wow — thank you.' I had no problem giving Alex the seed money to get started. I believe in Alex and his abilities to grow his business into something profitable. Soon, you'll see the name everywhere — Niles Custom Guitars."

THE JUDGES ON ALEX

There are a million ways to impress people with your business idea, but how many entrepreneurs can say they do it with an amp and a split jump? Wow! Alex's charisma is as electric as his guitars. When he started by telling us that he would capture 10 percent of the world's custom electric guitar market, we listened up. It's good to be confident, but it's also wise to think carefully before making a bold claim such as this.

Niles Custom Guitars are very high quality. Their craftsmanship is exceptional, and this will distinguish them in the marketplace. The guitars are made one at a time, and we wondered, as his company grows, how Alex will meet the demand for lots of guitars at once. He will need to train employees and build a staff that can manufacture the guitars as well as he does himself.

This young man is smart, though. Getting a celebrity endorsement gives his guitars a high profile and puts them in front of people who will attract other notables to spread the news about Alex's brand and the uniqueness of his product.

ALEX'S ADVICE FOR ROCKING A BUSINESS

1. Don't let anybody dampen your willpower to aspire.

2. Take action. As strong as a dream may be, it will stay a dream unless you work to make it a reality.

3. Be confident in your product, innovation, service, or anything you may be selling.

4. Get an attitude. Not a bad attitude, or one that's for show-offs, but a positive attitude. Cultivate an internal belief that tells people you know you'll succeed.

5. But keep an open mind. A know-it-all lacks humility. Always consider ideas from other people.

6. Check your numbers. If you don't know your company's finances, you don't know jack.

7. Think ahead. Consider possibilities, what may or may not happen, and come up with plans to handle situations as they arise. There are many different ways to play the same song.

8. Passion is the key to profits. If you don't love what you're doing, it will eventually plateau and not go any higher.

9. Put yourself in your clients' shoes. Ask questions they may ask. Are the prices fair? Is this advertisement really selling me? Do I want to spend money on this product?

10. Learn from mistakes. Sometimes, when you hit a wrong note, you hear something right: It opens you up to a whole new approach you'd never have considered otherwise.

"IN FIVE YEARS, I WANT MY BUSINESS TO BE WORTH $50 MILLION."

CHAPTER 10

STAR ALUMNUS

Jasmine Lawrence

17

eden BODY WORKS

Williamstown, New Jersey

ometimes it pays to lose. For Jasmine Lawrence, her business first started by losing her hair. When Jasmine was 11 years old, she got a perm that made her hair fall out. She was devastated, and spent much of sixth grade crying and trying to cover up her head. "I took medications and went to all kinds of doctors to try to make my hair grow back. Nothing worked," Jasmine remembers.

Jasmine and her mom, April, set out on a mission to find a hair care product that could help. Every label they read on the bottles and tubes of gels and creams listed nothing but hard-to-pronounce chemicals — the same stuff that damaged Jasmine's hair in the first place. "I tried to find all-natural alternatives, but there were none that worked," says Jasmine.

Jasmine took a very slick approach to a prickly problem. She was desperate to make her hair grow back and determined to create safe, organic beauty products for everyone. To do this, Jasmine researched and experimented with organic products, and in the process stumbled onto a formula that had healing properties for damaged strands. "Slowly, my hair started coming back," she says. "I never thought, *This*

could make me millions of dollars. I was really just thinking, *Yes! I'm not bald anymore!"*

With a new head of tresses and lots of self-confidence, Jasmine entered a business contest as part of BizCamp, a NFTE summer program. But she wasn't presenting her hair oil. She had also designed a line of decorative headbands to which she'd glued rhinestones and other glittery elements. The name of her company was Sweat 'N Style.

The concept was an intriguing one, but not a winner in the eyes of the contest judges. Also, for the contest, Jasmine didn't have enough business know-how to get started in the best possible way. Her hair was all there, but this time she lost the business competition. "My business plan was terrible," she admits.

None of this stopped Jasmine, who was still eager to launch a winning company. "I thought, *Why start from scratch when I have a great product I can sell right now?"*

While she was a student at Williamstown High School, Jasmine took everything she'd learned about being an entrepreneur and quickly turned her oil into opportunity. She revamped her business plan, clearly citing the cost of goods sold, return on investment, and strategies for future growth. With this new know-how, Jasmine launched Eden Body Works, a company that makes natural beauty products for the hair, body, and home.

Black Enterprise magazine, a publication for business professionals, nominated Jasmine for their "Teenpreneur of the Year" award.

Again, Jasmine lost, this time to a girl who made bumper stickers.

But this second loss was just what Jasmine needed to ultimately win big. The *Black Enterprise* exposure put Jasmine's product in front of women who wanted it badly — people like her who'd been burned by chemical hair relaxers.

Word spread fast about Eden Body Works, landing Jasmine a spot on *The Oprah Winfrey Show*!

"Within hours of the show airing, orders came in, hundreds at a time," Jasmine remembers. With her mom, she shipped out thousands of packages a day. Together they worked long shifts, barely even taking a moment to sleep, so that they could fulfill their orders. Boxes piled high in their living room, ready to be sent to customers all over the nation.

Based on the overwhelming response to Jasmine's appearance on *Oprah*, her mom made a major life change: She quit her job and came to work for her daughter. "My mom was willing to sacrifice anything for me," Jasmine says with gratitude.

Now the two enterprising women run a company that's taking home prizes — and profits. Jasmine says, "Working with Mom has been fun, and hard. I can't just fire her when I feel like it!" The two share a true partnership.

Jasmine recently struck a deal with Whole Foods Market, which carries her line of bath salts. She's also negotiated an arrangement with Wal-Mart. With distribution through two major American retailers, Jasmine's company has already achieved a level of success that most start-ups can only dream

of. As one of the most successful teenage entrepreneurs in the country, nobody can call this young lady a loser: The Jersey girl has hit the jackpot!

WORKING FOR BODY WORKS

JASMINE'S MOM, APRIL

"I remember taking Jasmine to the store to find products that would help her hair grow back after the perm disaster. All she kept saying was, 'No more chemicals, Mom!' When she lost the business contest for her Sweat 'N Style headbands, she

got all fired up to make a comeback. I look at Jasmine, who is one of my four daughters, and I get so inspired. Working with her has been wonderful, but we've had our moments. I can be a dictator at times. It's hard for any mom not to tell her child how to do things. But then I think about the expression, 'Mind your own business,' and I realize Jasmine has been doing that successfully for several years, without any help from me!

"And now I have the privilege of working for *her.* How many mothers can brag about calling their daughter the boss?"

STEVE MARIOTTI, NFTE FOUNDER, ON JASMINE

"Jasmine Lawrence is, without question, one of the greatest entrepreneurs I've seen in twenty-eight years. She has leadership ability and charisma. As a business owner, Jasmine has the entire package."

JASMINE'S KEY STRATEGY FOR MAKING BUSINESS WORK

As a former contestant and now successful entrepreneur, Jasmine has learned many lessons about business ownership. She agrees with the Top Ten tips offered by those NFTE competitors following in her footsteps. As a businesswoman on the rise, Jasmine advises giving back to the community. Volunteer your time and talent to help others. This is a key way to infuse your business with fresh ideas and new energy. As the saying goes, you can do well by doing good.

Seek out opportunities for volunteerism with schools, hospitals, libraries, and organizations that need a helping hand, advice, or expertise that you may have. Remember that no job is too small or "beneath" someone who can help. Because of your unique business experience, you have something to offer that no one else does. Lending a hand often yields gifts to the volunteer as much as to those who are being helped. Take this gift and pass it on.

CHAPTER 11

THE JUDGES DEBATE, DELIBERATE, DECIDE...

You've met the contenders — as well as a former contestant who didn't even come close to winning a national competition but still managed to create a business with profit projections in the millions! The decision was now in the hands of the judges. They'd narrowed it down to the top three, and among these, selected a grand prize winner.

Who would walk away with ten grand?

Here's the judges' wrap-up: All of the contestants were staggeringly impressive. We don't think we could have done any of this when we were teenagers ourselves. Their presentations were excellent, most of them knew their numbers, and they had some really unique ideas for business ventures.

But the question we asked ourselves was this: Who among these kids had *all* the right stuff — a scalable business, great presentation skills, and a solid grasp of the finances involved in running a company? And which one offered something that's a truly unique enterprise? It's one thing to be able to talk about your company well, but at the end of the day, it's the product or service that must be able to stand on its own, to prosper financially and commercially.

It was a challenge to choose one of these teens over another, and it was even tougher to decide who would take home the brass ring. Prize money of $10,000 is a substantial chunk of cash. If any of us were writing one of these kids a check from our own personal bank account, we'd want to make sure that the $10,000 was going to grow into a number that had a lot more zeros and another comma or two in its total.

Each and every one of these budding entrepreneurs was excellent. They should all feel very proud of themselves and their accomplishments. There's no doubt these kids are all on the road to success. The main thing they'll need to remember is to stay confident and focused on their goals. To always look forward, and to never say die. That's how the best businesses fly the highest.

HOW'D I DO?

One of the hardest parts about participating in any competition that involves giving a presentation, and whose winner is based on the opinions of others, is that you don't really know where you stand. It's like trying out for the school play, thinking you've aced the audition, then finding out you'll be playing a background tree! Or sometimes the opposite happens: You're convinced that you bombed the tryouts, only to discover that your spotlight is waiting!

Here's what the contestants learned from the competition, and what they thought about their chances to win.

TATYANA BLACKWELL, JUST CHEER UNIFORMS

"I'll be fine with whatever happens. I know that I'll always be a winner. I'm a strong black woman."

JESSICA CERVANTES, POPSY CAKES

"There were some amazing competitors. I speak really, really fast, and I think that was a mistake. Everyone's always telling me to slow down. I hope this didn't hurt my chances."

GABRIEL ECHOLES & RODNEY WALKER, FOREVER LIFE MUSIC & VIDEO PRODUCTIONS

RODNEY

"If you'd asked me a couple of months back, I would have told you we wouldn't make it to this point. We're the top competitors out of a total of 24,000. That's already an accomplishment. This experience has taught me that I can do anything."

GABRIEL

"I had been telling Rodney it was all going to come. I had no doubts we'd make it as far as we did."

MACALEE HARLIS, JR., MAC SHIELDS

"The judges asked a lot of tough questions, and there were a lot of good ideas out there — ideas that I really liked. I thought it was going to be close. That's what I expected from the beginning."

SHAN SHAN HUANG, CHARGER STATION

"I would like to have more challenges in life, and now, after competing in this contest, I'm ready."

AMANDA LOYOLA, ECODOG TREATS LLC

"At one point when the questions got tough, I looked at my parents, and then the timer, and blocked out everyone in the room. What I learned from this competition is that I'm a very sore loser! A hard lesson that I hope doesn't come into play."

WILLIAM MACK AND JA'MAL WILLS, J&W SENSATIONS

WILLIAM

"This has been a long journey. I've already shed some tears."

JA'MAL

"My main goal is to use what I've learned to stay in school, and to do well. I've already done that. So I'm already a winner."

ROBBIE MARTIN, THE DEAF ACADEMY

"When I was younger, many people thought I'd be a failure. I've now proved to them that I can be a success."

ALEXANDER NILES, NILES CUSTOM GUITARS

"Sometimes I'm a little too overconfident. I hope this didn't come across the wrong way."

CAST YOUR VOTE

Now it's your turn to choose a winner. *You* be the judge. Because every product is really judged by the people who buy it and use it.

Based on everything you've read about these amazing contestants and what they have to offer, put yourself in the judges' seats. But also think like the everyday consumer that you are.

On a separate piece of paper, list all the teens. Ask yourself if you would buy their product or use their service, or if you know someone who would. Which one of the NFTE competitors has everything you'd want in a business if you were the one handing over a bundle of money to get their company started?

Rank the contestants in order of preference.

Single out the top three.

The decision awaits.

See if you agree.

Just like at the Oscars, the NFTE winners' names were sealed in an envelope that was handed over to the judges. Steve Mariotti, NFTE founder, passed the envelope to Amy Rosen, the CEO and President of NFTE, who would announce the winner.

At that moment, the room was as quiet as the library on the day before final exams. Then the screech of the mic announced the good news.

THIRD PLACE . . .

Amanda Loyola, whose EcoDog Treats are muzzle-licking, organic snacks to help pooches munch to good health.

SECOND PLACE . . .

Rodney Walker and Gabriel Echoles, the video-hip co-CEOs who are making special memories last.

AND THE GRAND PRIZE
WINNER IS . . .
JUST A PAGE AWAY!

Jessica cervantes,

the Popsy Cakes creator who's bringing sweet-on-a-stick to everyone who loves desserts that are fun and yummy!

When Jessica heard the news, she was superpsyched — and surprised. And when she accepted the check in the amount of $10,000 (that's a lot of dough!), she knew her Popsy Cakes could now rise to even greater heights.

"We had a BIG discussion," says one of the judges. "We all felt that Rodney gave the most impressive presentation, but the Popsy Cakes were the most backable, bankable product."

So, there it is. After hours of planning, sweating, fretting, and sighing, these ten kids all came out with new ideas for moving their businesses forward and taking their enterprises to the next frontier. The NFTE competition was over — until next year. . . .

WHERE ARE THEY NOW?

THE CONTESTANTS ONE YEAR AFTER
THE COMPETITION

TATYANA BLACKWELL continues to R-I-S-E and shine as a business owner. Since the NFTE competition, she has worked hard on her school studies while at the same time perfecting her business model for Just Cheer and looking for ways to further distinguish her company. The budding entrepreneur has spent much of her post-NFTE time researching fabric manufacturers, garment production companies, and creators of cool stuff like glitter and tassels to add to her uniforms.

Several high schools have expressed interest in her "flashy-hot" skirts and tops, and the Just Cheer name just keeps on collecting fans.

JESSICA CERVANTES has been hard at work ever since she won the NFTE competition! Jessica has patented Popsy Cakes and registered a trademark for the name. She is working on several contracts with party planners and banquet halls.

The media has come calling, too. Jessica has been featured in several newspapers, along with *SOBeFiT*, *Florida Trend*, and *City & Shore* magazines.

Even with all of this attention, Jessica is studying hard at college. She is enrolled at Miami Dade College, where she's studying biomedical engineering, and hopes to become a corporate lawyer.

Macalee Harlis, Jr., is a student at Florida Atlantic University. He's still on the road to entrepreneurship, has revamped his business plan, and is creating a new prototype for MAC Shields to make his company even more appealing to investors.

Macalee recently won NFTE's Entrepreneur of the Year Award, an honor different than the one given at the National Youth Entrepreneur Challenge. Macalee also attended NFTE's Advanced Entrepreneurship Seminar, a weeklong summer program in New York City. After he earns his bachelor's degree, Macalee hopes to enroll in medical school, where he will study ophthalmology or optometry.

Shan Shan Huang attends the College of the Holy Cross in Massachusetts. College has been a great test-market for Shan Shan, who's looking for ways to make her Charger Stations available to as many students as possible so that she can solicit feedback from them.

Shan Shan's association with NFTE has been a good one. She is the recipient of a NFTE scholarship. She was also awarded the Delta Dental of Massachusetts Lubinger Scholarship.

Shan Shan hopes to get a job with an American company

that has an international reach so that she can return to China and live close to her extended family and her friends.

Amanda Loyola, one the youngest NFTE finalists, is still a high school student in New York City. She recently worked as an intern at J.P. Morgan, where she honed her business know-how and learned the ins and outs of a corporate environment.

Amanda's EcoDog Treats have gotten her attention on the *Today* show and Fox News. She's also been featured in the *Daily News*, a New York City newspaper, and *Seventeen* magazine.

Amanda plans on attending college and graduate school.

William Mack and Ja'Mal Wills have continued to work as a team on their lotion enterprise. They're both still in high school, with plans to attend college.

This team has been focusing on innovative marketing strategies for their J&W Sensations and has developed creative ways of reaching new clients. Their work has paid off. The OppenheimerFunds purchased 150 bottles of J&W Sensations lotion to use in their gift bags for a volunteer event.

Robbie Martin has been enjoying his time as a student at Gallaudet University in Washington, D.C. He is the recipient of Gallaudet's Leadership Scholarship, a true testament to Robbie's ability to guide others.

Robbie has continued his work with young people in the deaf and hearing communities, teaching them sign language. During his summers off from school, Robbie works with children at Bristol Community College's Kids College program. This has been great training for the future of The Deaf Academy, which he plans to continue in full force once he's graduated from college.

Alex Niles is a student at Dr. Michael M. Krop Senior High School in Miami. In addition to being a business owner, Alex has dreams of becoming a successful musician. He purchased an amazing acoustic Gibson guitar and has written several songs, which he hopes will be big hits someday soon.

Niles Custom Guitars is still Alex's passion. He spends every moment of his spare time crafting, upgrading, and painting his custom instruments.

Alex has enjoyed radio and television interviews, and his smiling face has appeared in many newspaper and magazine articles. After he finishes college, Alex wants to hit the road and tour with the instruments he loves most — his six-stringed sweethearts.

Rodney Walker is an honor student at Morehouse College in Atlanta. He and Gabe decided to make their business a solo endeavor as Gabe devotes precious time to his family.

Forever Life & Music Video Productions is going strong

at Morehouse, where Rodney is running the business while being a student. At school, he makes videos of college events and special occasions. Rodney's time spent on his business has counted toward his work-study program, so he's successfully been able to balance entrepreneurship with continuing his education.

Rodney has been highlighted in *The New York Times*, *The Chicago Sun-Times*, and *N'Digo* magazine. He's also been featured on National Public Radio, Plum TV, and ABC News.

THE QUIZ

DO YOU HAVE WHAT IT TAKES TO LAUNCH YOUR OWN BUSINESS?

Now that you've read the amazing stories of the young entrepreneurs in this book, you know what it takes to start your own business.

But could you do it? Could you come up with a winning business proposal? Could you draft a plan, create a prototype of your product, research your target market? Could you get past the judges and qualify for the top ten?

Whether you're an artist, fashion fanatic, or computer whiz, you probably have a business idea brewing. That's a good beginning, but you'll need to go further if you want your brainstorm to become a reality.

Here's a fun quiz that can help you get started by showing you some basic facts about your personality and how you handle business situations. As you answer the questions, think about the kids you've just met in this book. In what ways have they inspired you to think about challenges and opportunities? Your answers will reveal if you have what it takes to be the boss of your own empire.

To keep your book looking new — and to make it available for passing on to a friend — record your answers on a separate piece of paper. For each question, mark down the answer that best represents how you would respond.

1. You're at a party and a friend tells you that the guy in the expensive-looking suit recently invested in another friend's business. You:

a) Race over to him, introduce yourself, and tell him every detail of your business idea while asking if he'd be interested in investing in you.

b) Ask your friend to introduce you. When he does, hand the potential investor your business card and politely ask whether you might call him sometime to present him with your business plan.

c) Decide that it's probably not a good idea to bother the man at a party. After all, he's here to relax. Maybe you'll run into him again somewhere else.

2. Your boss puts you in charge of researching office supply stores and choosing the one that you think would be best for the company to use. Your response:

a) Yes! Finally, a chance to show the boss what you're made of — plus, you'll be able to sneak a few of those supplies away for your own business.

b) You're terrified. This is more responsibility than you really want. What if you make a mistake and cost the company a lot of money? You don't want to look bad.

c) You're excited. This is a good opportunity to impress your boss and also learn how to compare and negotiate with suppliers — something you'll need to do for your own business.

3. You're already going to school full-time when you're offered a part-time job that's in the same field as the business you want to start when you graduate next year. You:

a) Take the job, after talking with your student adviser about how to juggle your schedule so it will fit. The experience and the contacts you'll develop will be invaluable when you start your business.

b) Take the job. In fact, you ask for extra hours so you can finally start making some real money. Who needs sleep?

c) Turn down the job. School is hard enough without working, too. You don't want your grades to suffer.

4. You're offered a job as a survey-taker for a marketing firm. The job pays really well but will require you to talk to a great many people. You:

a) Take the job. You like people and this is a good way to practice getting to know what consumers want.

b) Pass on the job. Just the thought of approaching strangers makes you queasy.

c) Take the job so you can conduct some market research of your own by also asking the people you survey what they think about your business idea.

5. Your last job paid well and was interesting but required you to put in long hours and sometimes work on the weekend. Your response:

a) You put in the extra hours without complaint, but mainly because you felt that the rewards were worth it.

b) You went a little overboard and worked yourself into a state of exhaustion. Moderation is not your strong suit.

c) You quit. You are strictly a nine-to-fiver. Work is definitely not your life!

6. You are such a good guitar player that friends keep offering to pay for you to give them lessons. Your response:

a) You spend some bucks to run a six-week ad in the local paper announcing that you are now available to teach, at the same rate that other established teachers in the area charge.

b) You start teaching a few friends to see how it goes. You ask them what they are willing to pay and what they want to learn.

c) You give a few friends some lessons but refuse to take any money.

7. Your best friend has started a business designing websites. He needs help because the business is really growing. He offers to make you a partner in the business even though you consider yourself "computer illiterate." Your response:

a) You jump in, figuring you'll learn the ropes soon enough.

b) You ask your friend to keep the partnership offer open but first to recommend a class you can take to get your skills up to speed.

c) You pass on the offer — you don't see how you can work in a business you know nothing about.

OK! NOW YOU ARE READY TO ANALYZE YOUR ANSWERS. JUST READ ON.

ADD IT ALL UP

DO YOU (OR DO YOU *NOT*) HAVE WHAT IT TAKES?

Scoring

1.	2.	3.
a = 2	a = 2	a = 1
b = 1	b = 0	b = 2
c = 0	c = 1	c = 0

4.	5.	6.
a = 1	a = 1	a = 2
b = 0	b = 2	b = 1
c = 2	c = 0	c = 0

7.

a = 2

b = 1

c = 0

12 to 14 Points: You're a natural risk-taker and can handle a lot of stress. These are important characteristics an entrepreneur needs to be successful. You are willing to work hard but have a tendency to throw caution to the wind a little too easily. Save yourself from that tendency by carefully evaluating your business and personal decisions. In your enthusiasm, don't forget to look at what your decisions cost you. These are the costs of giving up the next best opportunity

that you could take with your time and money. You could go to school instead of starting a business, for example. But giving up going to school and the potential drawbacks of that decision could cost you in the long run.

6 to 11 Points: You strike an excellent balance between being a risk-taker and someone who carefully evaluates decisions. An entrepreneur needs to be both. You are also not overly motivated by the desire to make money, and that's good. You understand that a successful business will require hard work and some sacrifice before the rewards start rolling in. To make sure that you are applying your natural drive and discipline to the best possible business opportunity, carefully weigh the pros and cons of the business you are interested in starting.

5 Points or Fewer: You're a little cautious for an entrepreneur, but that will probably change as you learn more about how to run a business. You're concerned with financial security and may not be eager to put in the long hours required to get a business off the ground. This doesn't mean you won't succeed as an entrepreneur; just make sure that whatever business you decide to start is the business of your dreams, so that you will be motivated to make it a success. When considering entrepreneurship, choose a business that you believe has the best shot at providing you with both the financial security and the motivation you require.

WHAT DOES IT ALL MEAN?

Here are definitions of some of the business terms used in this book, and others that you'll need to know when starting a company.

360° MARKETING Approach to marketing that communicates with customers from all directions; it blends low-tech and high-tech methods to carry a message in as many ways as possible.

A

ACCOUNTS PAYABLE Amount of money a business owes to its suppliers for purchases made on credit.

ACCOUNTS RECEIVABLE Amount of money owed to a business by its customers for credit sales.

ACTIVE LISTENING Listening consciously and responding in ways that improve communication.

AFFILIATE MARKETING Process used by website owners who sell items from another store and take a percentage of the profits.

APPRENTICESHIP Internship in which a technical or trade skill is taught.

ASSET Everything owned by the business that has a monetary value.

B

BALANCE SHEET Financial statement that summarizes the assets and liabilities (debts) of a business.

BANK DEBT RATIO Your monthly income compared to your debts.

BARGAINING IN GOOD FAITH An honest intention to resolve differences in a way that is acceptable to all.

BARTER FINANCING Trading of items or services between businesses.

BOOTSTRAPPING Starting a business by yourself without any outside investment.

BRAND Marketing strategy that can create an emotional attachment to your product(s).

BRAND EQUITY Perceived monetary value of a brand.

BREAK-EVEN ANALYSIS Examination of the income statement that identifies the break-even point for a business.

BREAK-EVEN POINT Point at which the total at the bottom of the income statement is zero because the business has sold exactly enough units for sales to cover expenses.

BREAK-EVEN UNITS Number of units of sale a business needs to sell to arrive at the break-even point.

BURN RATE Rate at which a company spends cash to cover overhead costs without generating a positive cash flow.

BUSINESS ETHICS Moral principles applied to business issues and actions.

BUSINESS PLAN Statement of your business goals, the reasons you think these goals can be met, and how you are going to achieve them.

C

CALCULATED RISK Risk in which potential costs and benefits are carefully considered before starting a business.

CASH FLOW Money received minus what is spent over a specified period of time.

CASH FLOW STATEMENT Financial document that records inflows and outflows of cash when they actually occur.

COLD CALL Sales call to someone not known, and without prior notice; also called canvassing.

COLLATERAL Property or assets pledged to a bank to protect the investment of the lender.

COMPETITIVE ADVANTAGE Something that puts your business ahead of the competition.

COMPETITIVE INTELLIGENCE Data you collect about your competitors.

COPYRIGHT Exclusive right to perform, display, copy, or distribute an artistic work.

COST OF GOODS SOLD (COGS) Variable expense that is associated with each unit of sale, including the cost of materials and labor used to make the product or provide the service.

COST-BASED PRICING Pricing method that sets a product's price based on what it costs the business to provide it.

D

DAMAGES Payment to reimburse an injured party for loss.

DEBT CAPITAL Money obtained by a business through a loan.

DEBT FINANCING Obtaining money by borrowing it, thereby increasing your company's debt.

DEBT RATIO Ratio of a business's total debt divided by its total assets.

DEBT-TO-EQUITY RATIO Ratio of the total debts (liabilities) of a business divided by its owner's equity.

DIRECT COMPETITOR Business in your market that sells a product or service similar to yours.

DISTRIBUTION CHAIN Series of steps through which products flow into or out of a business. Also referred to as a distribution channel.

E

E-COMMERCE Process of buying and selling goods online.

ECONOMICS OF ONE UNIT Calculation of the profit (or loss) for each unit of sale made by a business.

ECONOMY OF SCALE Cost reduction made possible by spreading costs over a larger volume.

EMERGENCY FUND Amount of money a business should have available in the first three to six months for the emergencies that often arise when a company is just beginning. Cash saved to cover personal expenses for at least three months.

ENTERPRISE Another name for business.

ENTREPRENEUR Someone who creates and runs their own business.

ENTREPRENEURIAL Thinking or acting like an entrepreneur.

ENTREPRENEURIAL MIND-SET Mental attitude common to entrepreneurs that typically includes an optimistic, "can-do" outlook and the personal ambition necessary to create a business.

EQUITY CAPITAL Money obtained by a business from an investor in exchange for a share of ownership (equity) in the business.

ETHICS Set of moral principles that govern decisions and actions.

EXTERNAL SALES Sales obtained by hiring another company, or an outside individual, to do the selling for you.

F

FAIR USE Doctrine that provides for the limited quotation of a copyrighted work without permission from or payment to the copyright holder.

FINANCING Raising money for a business.

FISCAL YEAR Any 12-month period you choose to treat as a year for accounting purposes.

FIXED EXPENSE Expense that isn't affected by the number of items a business produces.

FOCUS GROUP Small number of people who are brought together to discuss a particular problem, product, or service.

G

GENERAL JOURNAL Accounting record that shows all the transactions of the business.

GENERAL PARTNERSHIP Partnership in which all partners have unlimited liability.

GLOBAL ECONOMY Flow of goods and services around the whole world.

GOODWILL Business term that encompasses the intangible positive aspects of a business, such as location, employee knowledge and skills, brand awareness, intellectual property, relationships with suppliers and customers, and reputation in the community and the industry.

GREEN COMPANY Company that adopts business practices aimed at protecting or improving the environment.

H

HARVESTING Exiting a business and gaining the value of the business in cash as one leaves.

I

IMPLIED CONTRACT Contract made when the parties' actions demonstrate their agreement.

IMPORTING Business activity in which goods and services are brought into a country from foreign suppliers.

INCOME STATEMENT Financial document that summarizes a business's income and expenses over a given time period and shows whether the business made a profit or took a loss. Also called a profit and loss statement.

INCORPORATE To set up a corporation in accordance with the laws of the particular state where the business is located.

INDIRECT COMPETITOR Business that sells a different product or service from yours but fills the same customer need or want.

INTELLECTUAL PROPERTY Artistic and industrial creations of the mind; legal rights to such content.

INTERNAL AUDIT Audit performed by an accountant hired by a company to check their books.

INTERNAL SALES Sales obtained by you or your employees who sell your products/services exclusively.

INTERPERSONAL SKILLS Skills used by people as they interact with others, particularly in a one-on-one setting.

INVENTORY MANAGEMENT Process of keeping track of the items for sale, storing them, and shipping orders.

INVENTORY SYSTEM Process for counting and tracking inventory so inventory value can be calculated.

INVESTING ACTIVITIES In relation to the statement of cash flow, these involve buying assets that will last more than one year.

J

JUST-IN-TIME (JIT) INVENTORY SYSTEM System in which the goal is to maintain just enough inventory to keep the business operating, with virtually no inventory kept in storage.

L

LICENSE To provide rights to use intellectual property. Legal document issued by the government that allows a business to provide a regulated product or service.

LIMITED LIABILITY COMPANY Legally defined type of business ownership that has properties of both a corporation and a partnership, and which is often well-suited to single-owner companies.

LIMITED PARTNERSHIP Partnership in which at least one partner has limited liability for the debts of the business.

LIQUIDATION Process in which the tangible assets of a business are sold.

LIQUIDITY Ability to convert assets into cash. Ease of converting a noncash asset (such as a business) into cash.

M

MARKET RESEARCH Organized way to gather and analyze information needed to make business decisions.

MARKET SHARE Percentage of a given market population that is buying a product or service from a particular business. Percentage of the total sales captured by a product or a business in a particular market.

MARKETING MIX "Recipe" for reaching and keeping customers that combines five marketing elements called the Five P's: people, product, place, price, and promotion.

MARKETING PLAN Detailed guide with two primary parts: marketing goals and strategies for reaching those goals.

MARKUP Price increase imposed by each link in a distribution chain or channel.

MARKUP PRICE Price created when a retailer adds an additional amount to the cost of a wholesale product to make a profit.

N

NEGOTIATION Process in which two or more parties reach an agreement or solve a problem through communication.

NET WORTH Total assets minus total liabilities according to a company's balance sheet. Also referred to as book value or owner's equity.

NONPROFIT CORPORATION Legally defined type of business ownership in which the company operates not to provide profit for its shareholders but to serve the good of society.

NONPROFIT ORGANIZATION Organization that operates solely to serve the good of society.

O

OBSOLESCENCE Process of becoming obsolete, which means no longer useful or desired.

OPERATIONAL PLAN Plan that details the everyday activities that will achieve the long-range goals of a business venture.

OPERATIONS Everyday activities that keep a business running.

OPERATIONS MANAGEMENT Management of the everyday activities that keep a business running.

ORGANIC GROWTH Growth achieved by expanding a business internally—for example, adding new products or services for sale.

OUTSOURCING Hiring another company or individual to handle part of a business's everyday operations or to do special projects.

P

PARTNERSHIP Legally defined type of business organization in which at least two individuals share the management, profit, and liability.

PARTNERSHIP AGREEMENT Legal document that clearly defines how the work, responsibilities, rewards, and liabilities of a partnership will be shared by the partners.

PATENT Exclusive right to make, use, or sell a device or process.

PERMIT Legal document that allows a business to take a specific action.

PERSONAL SELLING Direct (person-to-person) effort made by a company's sales representatives to get sales and build customer relationships.

PRICE DISCRIMINATION Charging competing buyers different prices for the same product.

PRICE FIXING Competitors agreeing to set the price of goods or services, or the terms of business deals.

PRODUCT LIFE CYCLE Series of stages—introduction, growth, maturity, and decline—that a product may pass through while it is on the market.

PRODUCT MIX Combination of products that a business sells.

PRODUCT PLACEMENT When a company pays a fee to have a product displayed during a movie or television show.

PRODUCT POSITIONING Process of creating a strong image for your product; a way of influencing customers to distinguish your brand's characteristics from those of the competition.

PROFIT AND LOSS STATEMENT Another name for an income statement.

PROSPECT Person or company with many of the characteristics of the target market, including some key characteristics.

PROTOTYPE Model on which future reproductions of an invention are based.

Q

QUALITY CONTROL PROGRAM Program used by a business to ensure that its products or services meet specific quality standards.

QUICK RATIO Comparison of cash to debt, based on the concept that a business should have at least enough money on hand to pay its current debts.

QUOTA Limit on the quantity of a product that can be imported into a country.

R

RECALL Notice for customers to return a product that poses a risk of injury or illness.

REPEAT CUSTOMERS Customers who come back again and again.

REPLACEMENT COST Cost of replacing property at current prices.

RETURN ON INVESTMENT (ROI) Profit on an investment expressed as a percentage of the total invested.

RETURN ON SALES (ROS) Financial ratio calculated by dividing net profit by sales.

S

SAFETY STOCK Minimum amount of inventory kept to protect against a stock outage due to unusually high demand or unusually long lead times on delivery.

SALES FORECAST Prediction of the amount of future sales your company expects to achieve over a certain period of time.

SEED MONEY Another term for start-up capital or start-up investment.

STRATEGIC PLAN Plan that lays out a broad course of action to achieve a long-term goal, typically three to five years in the future.

SUPPLY AND DEMAND CURVE A graph that includes both a supply curve and a demand curve. Shows the relationship between prices and the quantities of a product or service that are supplied and demanded.

T

T-ACCOUNT Double-sided presentation that shows credits and debits.

TARGET MARKET Limited number of customers who are most likely to buy a specific product or service.

THIRD-PARTY TRANSACTION Exchange in which a third party collects the money from the buyer and then pays the seller.

TRADE SECRET Any information that a business or individual keeps confidential to gain advantage over competitors.

TRADE SHOW Convention where related businesses come to promote their products or services.

TRADEMARK Symbol that indicates that the use of a brand or brand name is legally protected and cannot be used by other businesses. A type of intellectual property.

U

UNIT OF SALE What a customer actually buys from you. It's the amount of product (or service) that you use to figure your operations and profit.

UNLIMITED LIABILITY When a business owner can be legally forced to use personal money and possessions to pay the debts of the business.

V

VARIABLE EXPENSE Expense that changes based on the amount of product or service a business sells.

VENTURE CAPITAL Money invested in a potentially profitable business by a specialized company whose purpose is to invest in start-ups.

VIRAL MARKETING Word-of-mouth promotion on the Internet.

VIRTUAL STOREFRONT Website that can list products, prices, payment terms, and shipping costs, as well as process orders.

VISION "Picture" of what you want the future to be.

VOLUME BUYING Purchasing a large quantity from a vendor, typically to take advantage of a quantity discount. Also referred to as buying in bulk.

W

WHOLESALER Business that buys goods in large quantities, typically from manufacturers, and resells them in smaller batches to retailers. Also referred to as a wholesaling business.

WORD OF MOUTH Verbal communications or publicity.

Z

ZONING LAWS Local laws that specify the types of development and activities — residential, commercial, industrial, or recreational — that can take place on particular pieces of property.

MORE JUDGES

NFTE enlisted many judges over several rounds of the National Youth Entrepreneurship Challenge. In addition to those featured in this book, others included:

Patricia Alper	President	Alper Portfolio Group
Andy Barfuss	Partner	Amper, Politziner & Mattia LLP
Cesar Bastidas	Manager, Sales	OFI
Brian Bedol	Founder	College Sports Network
Arthur Blank	Owner & CEO and Co-Founder	Atlanta Falcons and the Georgia Force; The Home Depot
Elon Boms	Managing Director	LaunchCapital
Michelle Brennan	Vice President, Strategic Accounts	OFI
Casey Budesilich	National Growth Director	Breakthrough Collaborative
Melissa Clayton	Assistant Vice President, Sales	OFI
Doug Douglass	Founding Managing Director	K2 Advisors
Bruce Dunbar	Senior Vice Corporate President, Communications	OFI
Rachael Fanopoulos	Assistant Vice President, Marketing	OFI
Charissa Fernandez	COO	TASC

Hazem Gamal	Vice President, Sales	OFI
Josh Green	CEO	Panjiva
Ray Hamel	Founder	Pure Encapsulations
Ken Heuer	Partner	Kidd Company
Amy Houston	SVP, Strategy	Robin Hood Foundation
Alan Kersh	Senior Vice President	TGM Associates
Lisa Lamentino	Vice President, Marketing	OFI
Rhonda Lauer	CEO	Foundations, Inc.
Meena Mansharamani	Former Senior Vice President, Innovations & Insights	PepsiCola, NA
Ron Morris	Director, Entrepreneurial Studies Program	Duquesne University
Lisette Nieves	Executive Director	Year Up NYC
Maria Pena	Americas Leader of Entrepreneurship	Ernst & Young
Stan Pottinger	CEO	Pottinger Nichols Media Group, LLC
Richard Ramsey	President and CEO	LEAD
Freda Richmond	Executive Director	College Summit, NYC
Steven Sanders	Chairman & CEO	First Genesis Financial Group

Dan Schroeder	Partner, Business & Risk Advisory Services	Amper, Politziner & Mattia LLP
Dia Simms	General Manager	Blue Flame
Lari Stanton	Former CEO and Chairman	Aris-Isotoner, Inc.
Marty Telles	Senior Vice President, Marketing	OFI
William Tkacs	Managing Partner	Vested Capital
Elaine Villas-Obusan	Assistant Vice President, Marketing	OFI
Carole Wacey	Executive Director	MOUSE
Emily Weiss	Partner	Accenture
Beth Westvold	Managing Director	BlackRock
Leah Williams	CEO	Strategies
Sean Williamson	Manager, Corporate Communications	OFI

Since 1987, the Network for Teaching Entrepreneurship (NFTE) has reached over 186,000 young people and currently has programs in 21 states as well as 13 countries outside the United States.

NFTE provides entrepreneurship education programs to young people from low-income communities. The NFTE goal is to empower young people, many of whom struggle in school, and to change their lives through entrepreneurship education.

NFTE's program offices are located in Baltimore; Bay Area; Chicago; Greater Dallas; Fairchester (Fairfield County, CT, and Westchester County, NY); Greater Los Angeles; New England; New York Metro; Pittsburgh; South Florida; Greater Washington, D.C.; and Philadelphia.

HOW NFTE WORKS

NFTE programs take place in middle and high schools, in after-school settings, and via NFTE's summer BizCamps. NFTE begins with an intensive four-day training for professional teachers and youth workers that takes them through NFTE's award-winning entrepreneurship curriculum and provides ideas on how to make the lessons compelling for their students. Once trained, our teachers guide students through the "ABCs of Entrepreneurship," including the

concepts of ownership, opportunity recognition, marketing, finance, product development, and competitive advantage. NFTE teachers receive ongoing support and training from NFTE staff.

Each NFTE student works toward completing a business plan, and top students are invited to participate in a regional competition. Following their completion of the NFTE program, students have access to our alumni services, which include advanced training, mentoring programs, workshops, and access to awards and scholarship opportunities, in hopes that the lessons they learned as NFTE students will carry through in their future endeavors.

HOW YOU CAN HELP

NFTE relies on the generosity of corporations, foundations, and individuals to keep our programs running across the country and around the world. If you would like to make a donation to help more low-income kids turn their lives around by participating in NFTE, visit the NFTE website at www.nfte.com.

Volunteers play a crucial role in NFTE's programs. You can share your knowledge and love of business in a variety of ways — by running a workshop in your area of expertise, becoming a business plan coach to help a student fine-tune their business plan, or being a judge at one of our business plan competitions. All of these opportunities require minimal time commitments but can make a huge difference in the life of a NFTE student.

FOR FURTHER READING:

Mariotti, Steve, with Tony Towle. *Entrepreneurship: Owning Your Own Future*. New York, NY: Prentice Hall, 2010.

Mariotti, Steve, with Tony Towle. *Entrepreneurs in Profile*. Franklin Lakes, NJ: Career Press, 2002.

WEBSITES

http://www.nfte.com
http://www.nftealumninetwork.com/

CONTRIBUTOR BIOS

Mary Mazzio, an award-winning director, Olympian, and former law firm partner, is Founder and CEO of 50 Eggs, LLC, an independent film production company. Mazzio wrote, directed, and produced the highly acclaimed, award-winning films *Lemonade Stories*, *Apple Pie*, and *A Hero for Daisy*. TEN9EIGHT is her newest documentary. Mazzio, an Olympic athlete (1992, Rowing), is a graduate of Mount Holyoke College and Georgetown Law School. The Schlesinger Library at Harvard University has requested all of Mazzio's papers for its collection. For more about Mazzio or her films, please log onto www.50eggs.com.

Amy Rosen is the President and CEO of NFTE, an organization that provides entrepreneurship education to young people from low income communities throughout the world, and she hosts competitions like those featured in this book. She is a nationally recognized expert in urban school system reform and champions her belief that all children should be given an opportunity to receive a high-quality education and the tools to find their own path to prosperity. She has been the recipient of many awards recognizing her accomplishments, and lives with her family in Montclair, New Jersey.

Andrea Davis Pinkney is the author of many acclaimed books for young people. She has written articles for *The New York Times*, *Essence*, *School Library Journal*, *Booklist*, and *Executive Female* magazines, among others. Pinkney was named one of the "25 Most Influential Black Women in Business" by *The Network Journal*, a publication for business professionals. She lives in New York City.

The photographs in the book were taken by **Richard Schultz,** who has been shooting professionally for almost 20 years and has worked on various projects all over the world. His images have been featured in many magazines, including *National Geographic*, *Time*, *Sports Illustrated*, *Vanity Fair*, and *Fortune*. He is a recipient of a World Press Photo Award as well as numerous Addy and Communication Arts awards. He currently lives in Barrington, Rhode Island, with his wife and two sons.

In America, a kid drop of high school every 9

Imagine if they didn't.

TEN9EIGHT
SHOOT FOR THE MOON
A MARY MAZZIO GIG   TEN9EIGHT.COM

50 EGGS PRESENTS TEN9EIGHT A MARY MAZZIO GIG
EDITED BY PAUL GATTUSO   DIRECTOR OF PHOTOGRAPHY RICHARD KLUG   MUSIC BY ALEX LASARENKO   STILL PHOTOGRAPHER RICHARD SCHULTZ
WRITER/DIRECTOR EXECUTIVE PRODUCER MARY MAZZIO

JOHN TEMPLETON FOUNDATION   KAUFFMAN   NFTE   50 EGGS FILMS   BET   AMC THEATRES
SUPPORTING SCIENCE-INVESTING IN THE BIG QUESTIONS   The Foundation of Entrepreneurship

TO ORDER THE FILM, FROM WHICH THIS BOOK WAS DERIVED,
PLEASE VISIT WWW.1098.COM OR CALL 1-877-98-DAISY.

LIGHTS, CAMERA, ACTION! THE NFTE COMPETITORS
WORK HARD, STAND TALL, POLISH THEIR
PRESENTATIONS — AND GO FOR THE WIN!

HOW SWEET IT IS! JESSICA'S MOM CONGRATULATES HER DAUGHTER AT THE FINALS.

PORTRAIT OF A MOGUL: JASMINE IS ONE OF THE MOST ACCOMPLISHED PARTICIPANTS IN NFTE'S HISTORY.

WHEN JASMINE AND HER MOM, APRIL, BECAME
BUSINESS PARTNERS, THEY SWUNG INTO ACTION.

THANKS TO HER EDEN BODY WORKS HAIR CARE PRODUCTS, JASMINE LAWRENCE IS TRESSED FOR SUCCESS.

CHIN UP: ALEX HAS GOT A LEVEL HEAD FOR BUSINESS.

CRAFTSMANSHIP AND COOL COLORS ARE
TRADEMARKS OF NILES CUSTOM GUITARS.

KID ROCKER ALEX NILES MAKES MUSIC — AND
MONEY — WITH HIS CUSTOM GUITARS.

EYES ON THE PRIZE: ROBBIE MARTIN LOOKS TOWARD
THE BRIGHT FUTURE OF HIS DEAF ACADEMY.

ROBBIE LETS HIS FINGERS DO THE TALKING,
DEMONSTRATING THE SKILL OF SIGN LANGUAGE.

JEANNE MARTIN, ROBBIE'S MOM, EMBRACES HER
SON'S SMARTS AND SENSE OF HUMOR.

SMOOTH-TALKING THE JUDGES: JA'MAL AND WILLIAM
MAKE THEIR PITCH.

THE TIES HAVE IT! JA'MAL AND WILLIAM DRESS THE
PART OF SUCCESSFUL BUSINESS OWNERS.

SAFETY FIRST! JA'MAL WILLS (LEFT) AND WILLIAM MACK (RIGHT) STRAP ON THE LAB GOGGLES BEFORE WHIPPING UP A BATCH OF THEIR J&W SENSATIONS ALL-NATURAL LOTIONS.

MADE BY HAND AND MADE WITH LOVE, IN AMANDA'S
OWN NYC KITCHEN: ECODOG TREATS.

A KISS FOR CONFIDENCE: MOM IS BY AMANDA'S SIDE
TO SUPPORT HER THROUGH THE COMPETITION.

TAKING IT TO THE STREETS, AMANDA LOYOLA GETS A CUSTOMER'S OPINION OF HER ECODOG TREATS.

FROM CHINA TO THE NFTE FINALS IN NEW YORK CITY;
SHAN SHAN HAS COME A LONG WAY.

FAMILY HELPS SHAN SHAN KEEP IT ALL IN BALANCE.

SHAN SHAN HUANG PROVES THAT BIG IDEAS COME
IN SMALL PACKAGES.

THE SHAPE OF THINGS TO COME: MACALEE SHOWS
OFF THE OPTICAL TECHNOLOGY OF HIS MAC SHIELDS.

HE'S GOT THE GOODS, AND HE'S GOT GAME: MACALEE
HARLIS HOLDS A PROTOTYPE OF HIS SHIELD.

RODNEY'S "TRIPLE S" STRATEGY FOR SUCCESS: SUIT
UP. SHOW UP. SMILE!

GABRIEL IS COOL, CALM, AND COLLECTED BEFORE
THE COMPETITION.

THEY'VE GOT EACH OTHER'S BACK, AND THEY SEE EYE-TO-EYE: CO-CEOS GABRIEL ECHOLES (LEFT) AND RODNEY WALKER (RIGHT) OF FOREVER LIFE MUSIC & VIDEO PRODUCTIONS.

TATYANA'S MOM IS ALWAYS CHEERING HER ON:
Y-O-U G-O, G-I-R-L!

AS CHEERLEADER-IN-CHIEF, TATYANA RARELY SITS STILL.

AS JUST CHEER'S PROFIT PROJECTIONS JUMP,
TATYANA BLACKWELL HAS PLENTY TO SMILE ABOUT.

SPEAKING TO THE MEDIA: JESSICA'S IN THE SPOTLIGHT.

READY FOR HER CLOSE-UP: JESSICA, POISED AND
PROFESSIONAL.

FROM THE DOCUMENTARY FILM

TEN9EIGHT

teen BUSINESS BLASTS OFF!

By **Andrea Davis Pinkney** and **Amy Rosen** • Photographs by **Richard Schultz**
Foreword by **Steve Mariotti**, Founder, Network for Teaching Entrepreneurship
Introduction by **Kim Myles** • Derived from the Film TEN9EIGHT
by **Mary Mazzio**, 50 Eggs Productions

SCHOLASTIC INC.
New York   Toronto   London   Auckland
Sydney   Mexico City   New Delhi   Hong Kong

With Special Thanks to

Creative Consultant Patricia Alper

●　　　　　●　　　　　●

ISBN 978-0-545-21877-1

Publisher's Note: The judges' opinions expressed herein are a composite drawn from their collective comments expressed in the film TEN9EIGHT, and based on commentary in that film. These judges' comments should not be deemed the sole or complete opinion of any individual or the companies with which they are affiliated.

10 9 8 7 6 5 4 3 2　　　　10 11 12 13 14

Printed in the U.S.A.　　23
First printing, January 2010

Book design by Kay Petronio